12/97

IPA, PHO, AND MSO DEVELOPMENTAL STRATEGIES

Building Successful Provider Alliances

IPA, PHO, AND MSO DEVELOPMENTAL STRATEGIES

Building Successful Provider Alliances

MARIA K. TODD

(co-published with the Healthcare Financial Management Association)

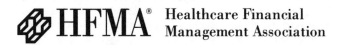 **HFMA**® Healthcare Financial Management Association

Educational Foundation

McGraw-Hill

New York   San Francisco   Washington, D.C.   Auckland   Bogotá
Caracas   Lisbon   London   Madrid   Mexico City   Milan
Montreal   New Delhi   San Juan   Singapore
Sydney   Tokyo   Toronto

Library of Congress Cataloging-in-Publication Data

Todd, Maria K.
    IPA, PHO, and MSO developmental strategies : building successful
provider alliances / Maria K. Todd.
        p.   cm.
    Includes bibliographical references and index.
    ISBN 0–7863–1119–3 (alk. paper)
    1. Group medical practice—United States   I. Title.
    [DNLM: 1. Independent Practice Associations—organization &
administration—United States.   2. Hospital–Physician Joint Ventures—
organization & administration—United States.   3. Contract
Services—organization & administration—United States.
    4. Financial Management.   W 130 AA1 T6i 1997]
    R729.5.G6T63   1997
    610′.65′0973—DC21   97-41389
                                                                 CIP

McGraw-Hill

A Division of The **McGraw·Hill** *Companies*

1 2 3 4 5 6 7 8 9 0 BKM / BKM 9 0 9 8 7

Printed and bound by Book-Mart Press, Inc.

This publication is designed to provide accurate and authoritative information in regard to the subject matter covered. It is sold with the understanding that neither the author nor the publisher is engaged in rendering legal,
accounting, or other professional service. If legal advice or other expert assistance is required, the services of a competent professional person
should be sought.
                —From a Declaration of Principles jointly adopted by a Committee
                        of the American Bar Association and a Committee of Publishers

McGraw-Hill books are available at special quantity discounts to use as
premiums and sales promotions, or for use in corporate training programs.
For more information, please write to the Director of Special Sales,
McGraw-Hill, 11 West 19th Street, New York, NY 10011. Or contact your
local bookstore.

This book is dedicated to my clients, my friends, and my family. For without the faith in my abilities and the opportunities and challenges they presented me this book could have never been written.

We Are All Angels With But One Wing
And We Can Fly
Only If We Embrace One Another.

Thank you!

ACKNOWLEDGMENTS

As I write this tonight, the eve of my fortieth birthday, I find new meaning in the phrase, *"Over the Hill!"* This book was by far the most difficult task I have ever committed to. It took over eighteen months to acquire some of the pieces from government sources, and overcome some of the hardest personal hurdles including the loss of my mother and my father becoming ill to the point of having to move him in with us.

The subject matter is well known to me, and I have participated in hundreds of seminars on IPA, PHO, and MSO development. I have consulted to some of the nation's finest minds in healthcare. However, committing it to writing with so many variables in each area was by far the hardest task to put on paper without becoming lost in the myriad of choices available in the design, implementation, and nomenclature of the different three letter acronyms (TLAs) and four letter acronyms (FLAs) of managed care. I am a firm believer that "It is not what you call the organization, it is what it is doing that matters most!" If you have seen one of the IPAs, PHOs, or MSOs, you have seen only one of them. The variations are endless! Putting these options to print is a task that I am glad is behind me.

In order to have accomplished this, I must admit that I did not achieve this alone. The team behind the writing of this book deserves much of the praise with me. First, the folks at McGraw-Hill Healthcare Education Group, namely Kristine Rynne, one of my closest professional associates and publisher. She has tried hard to assist in whatever way possible to make both the seminar series on *Managed Care Contracting and Negotiating* and the production of this book happen. Also, those professionals at the HFMA who co-published this and my previous book *The Managed Care Contracting Handbook,* for their patience and understanding with necessary extensions on manuscript deadline.

I also have to thank my computer technical support folks, Don Banka and Tim Echlard, and the guys at Comp USA for putting forth valiant efforts to keep me writing despite several setbacks of the computer kind (that is, hard drive crashes, blown motherboards, operating systems that chose not to work, and those nasty little people inside my computer who like to mess with my head! I know you are in there!). I am sure that my lost documents will turn up in heaven with the orphaned socks that the "dryer monster" has absconded with!

I also want to acknowledge my attorney friends Gerald A. Niederman, Esq., of Faegre and Benson, LLC in Denver, and Gabriel Imperato, Esq., of Broad and Cassel in Fort Lauderdale, for their open door to my questions both during the writing of this book and while working with clients. As a paralegal, I can only go so far with some information. These guys are wonderful, generous mentors and I appreciate them more than they know.

To the many fine physicians who have put their faith in my abilities as a consultant, and have made me proud of their efforts and their leadership; Maria Scouros, M.D., and her team in Houston, who has in the past three years gone from inexperienced president of a developing IPA and MSO to Board Member of the IPA Association of America. I am so proud of you, Maria! A special thank you to my extended family in Hawaii: Pat Chinn, M.D., Calvin Wong, M.D. and his lovely wife Susan Wong, Esq., Lockwood Young, M.D., Herb Chinn, M.D., Tim Owen, M.D., Dick De Journett, M.D., and the many other personalities that have shared their warmth with Tom and me and taught us the meaning of the true "Aloha Spirit." I will not forget the bar-b-q meeting at the beach house in Kailua, sitting cross-legged in our socks and bare feet in the living room talking about electronic medical records systems until the late evening. Your special kindness at the passing of my mother was very special to me and my family. I also want to thank Gene Nobles, M.D. (remember the late Claude Ledes, M.D. a wonderful man with an understanding of team leadership, I am sure that he is missed by many) and his team out in Memphis who jumped from the frying pan of development of an IPA into the fire of exclusive partnering with an HMO in its early stages, that takes guts! A special thank you to Bellur Ramanath, M.D., in San Antonio for allowing me to participate in and having the confidence in my abilities and the consultants I chose to help with his most unique dilemma as a pediatrician taking the sole capitated risk for over 7000 commercial and

Medicare lives—we both learned lessons that I have been able to share in this book. Also, a thank you for Chicagoland's United Eye Care Providers, especially the tenacious Steve Combs, O.D., and Marty Sikorski, O.D., for bestowing confidence in my abilities and my commitment to the group's success.

Some of the lessons learned that I shared in this book came from the more memorable experiences I have shared as a consultant. I will never forget Dan Shea, Psy.D., and his team of Texas psychotherapists, who taught me how to have fun during a retreat in a cabin in the snow, in the woods of east Texas in my socks explaining IPA/MSO development by the fireplace. While I am on the subject of psych, I cannot forget to mention a thank you to David Goldstein, M.D., and Mark Rhine, M.D., and friends, who taught me that there is life activity at 7:00am on Sunday mornings. Everyone who heard I was working on a Psychiatric PHO at that hour told me "I" needed a referral and they were not too far off . . . but it was worth it! To Howard Corren, M.D., Richard Patt, M.D., and the "chocolaholics anonymous" . . . Bruce Hayward, D.O., Leslie Cocoran, M.D., at Primary Care Physicians of Aurora, in Colorado, as well as founders Bill Solomon, M.D., Gerry Kirshenbaum, M.D., of Summit Physician Organization, in Colorado. I also send a thank you to the great folks in Coos Bay, Oregon, Bob Levy, M.D., and his Board of DOCS, Dr. Jim McKeown, who sent precious sentiments cards on the passing of my mother, and their "cohort of sorts," Monty Johnston (who promised to call daily if I had to do time in "doggy jail" on account of my felonious hounds). Every time I am in Oregon, you treat me like family. Last but not least, Steve Arter in San Diego and his Scottsdale team at *Interlink* and the group at Rothenberg and Associates with *EZ Cap* who are always there to help with answers about data development and management, have been gracious and generous with their time and effort for my MSO clients and to me. Without every one of these fine leaders and the projects which I have been involved with in the past few years, the memories, the firsthand experiences, and the material for this book would have never been possible. I was able to write in the "first person" relaxed conversational style as opposed to a boring didactic style found in so many books of a technical nature. I hope it makes you proud to know you have been a part of this endeavor with me.

A big thanks to Albert Hollway, President of The IPA Association of America for agreeing to the writing of the Foreword in spite of his busy travel and speaking schedule. Now I can get started writing that column for TIPS that I promised!

I need to extend a special thank you to my orthopedic surgeon, Robert R. Rokicki, M.D., our hand surgeon Louis H. Oster, M.D., and a team of wonderful massage therapists, namely Barry Drexler, and the talented practice group at Standley Lake Massage Therapy Clinic. You have kept me moving despite bilateral rotator cuff injuries, et al! I thank you and I am sure that the publishers thank you!

I also want to thank my family, including my Godfather, Nick Lopusznick, who always believed that someday my efforts would bring success, and told me so!

And finally, from the bottom of my heart, I want to thank the two people in my life who know more intimately than anyone what it took to accomplish the completion of the book throughout the last eighteen months. My friend of more than twenty-five years, my business and personal assistant, Mike Russe. Without his attention to detail, extra efforts, and friendship I would have never been able to keep on course despite all the personal and professional trials the last year and a half has presented me. I do not know that I could have ever accomplished this book without him being there for me. Last, but never least, I must thank (yes, still my significant other . . .) Tom Palizzi, my other (better) half, my confidant, my friend, new business partner, and my knight in shining armor. Tom would call frequently from work when he knew I would be writing to remind me to take breaks and rest my wrist and my eyes . . . and tidy up my office! Now I can straighten out my office, focus on him . . . and us . . . for a little while!

FOREWORD

The healthcare environment today dictates that physicians enhance the role they are playing in directing the physician groups, not only from the contracting perspective, but also from the management perspective. Physicians can no longer stand on the sidelines and permit other individuals to direct their fate. They must play a proactive role in ensuring that their voice is heard when policies are being set that will govern their livelihood. It is very easy to take a passive position and assume that others will direct the healthcare system in a manner which recognizes the crucial role of the physician. If this was ever true, it is definitely not true today. It is crucial that physicians seize control of all management aspects of today's healthcare delivery system. In order to do this, physicians must prepare themselves for management responsibilities just as diligently as they went about preparing themselves for their clinical roles. The health delivery systems in America, beyond any doubt, has no equal from a clinical perspective. America has the best trained clinical minds on this planet. This did not occur by accident rather it resulted from a sincere concern on the part of physicians as they prepared themselves for their clinical roles. The time has come for physicians to apply this same diligence to their role in directing the healthcare system. They must continue to be outstanding clinicians while acquiring management expertise. This management expertise can be acquired through utilizing a variety of resources. An understanding of the principles and concepts presented in this publication is one of many steps physicians must take as they prepare themselves for management roles. The author of this publication has presented many theories and principles that are crucial to the effective management of physician groups. I encourage physician managers to read this publication and become familiar with its contents and benefit from the experience of others outlined in this publication.

CONTENTS

INTRODUCTION

How It All Began

The setting is the local hospital, in the cafeteria. It is time for lunch. Both Dr. Williams and Dr. Jones are in line waiting for Maureen to serve up some of the hospital's infamous "mystery meat," something that would look more appropriate in a science lab experiment or a pathology specimen. Trying to avoid too much consideration of the delicious hospital cuisine, Dr. Williams turns to select a roll and some fat-free margarine and says to Dr. Jones, "Heard anything about that new IPA that some of the guys have been talking about?" "No, but then isn't that only for you primary care guys, anyway?" replies Jones, an orthopedic surgeon. As they make their way to the cashier, Williams adds, "Well, after all, the primary care guys control the referrals, so they should have the helm of the organization." While walking to the doctor's lounge, Jones responds, "I heard all that IPA stuff is not going to make a difference once the hospital gets the PHO up and running. And besides, if the hospital gets the PHO off the ground, I heard that any IPAs will be kind of moot because the managed-care contracting will be done at the PHO level."

Williams and Jones select seats at an eight-foot table, where other doctors are already sitting. Dr. MacAdams, a soon to be

1

retired obstetrician /gynecologist, says "I heard that the PHO is going to buy practices up from some of us. That suits me just fine, it will save me the hassle of finding a buyer when I retire, and, for now, all I have to do as a medical staff member is send a check to participate. Frankly, I wish all this managed-care stuff would just go away and leave me alone with my scalpel and new babies and their mothers." "This is not the medicine I came to practice!" Dr. Silverstein, an ENT, who finished residency only 6 months ago, seated opposite MacAdams says, "Sure, Mac, but how about us new guys? My overhead to gross ratio is at 65% these days. I have staff, personal expenses, and loans to pay off from school. I never learned this stuff, and yet I get envelopes full of offers to join this IPA, that PHO, this HMO, that PPO . . . seems everybody wants up-wards of at least a thousand bucks to join something or other!" Dr. Johnson, an anesthesiologist, looks up from his sandwich and asks, "What about us hospital-based guys? We take what is given to us when the hospital gets a contract for itself. Our needs are hardly ever represented by the hospital, just as radiology, ED, pathology and neonatal are not. I am not too sure that I want the PHO, a not-for-profit company representing my for-profit interests in con-tracting with these payors, but I do not know how to do this stuff, and I do not know who does to be honest with you!"

Dr. Beth Warner, a female family practitioner, who recently moved to the area from California looks up from her salad and adds to the commentary with, "It seems like maybe we should build an organization just for the physicians and partner equally with the hospital . . . maybe micro-manage ourselves through a physician organization that makes up the "P" in PHO. I am not sure that a not-for-profit PHO is the answer for me, but have you guys heard of the concept of the MSO? It's a management ser-vices organization. We had lots of 'em in California. Some bought practices, some did not. It kind of served as a centralized busi-ness entity for all of us. We each threw in some capital and be-came economically integrated. Because of the expense involved, we could share risk for profit or loss, own our own data, con-tracts, and practices." "Yea Beth, you can say that again! Mega-expense is more like it" said Silverstein. No, really guys . . . it does not take as much cash as you think! Sure the MSO costs a couple of million to start-up in the first year, but not all the money needs to be raised at once. And, these days, there are strategic partners, with venture capital to help, who are not connected to any insurance company or the hospital. They see the growth potential in healthcare these days and want a piece of the action" she added.

Sound familiar? It should! This scene is repeated in hospital dining rooms and hallways everywhere in America these days. Either the conversation did happen or is happening as we speak, and it may actually happen several times in one hospital over the course of a few years.

The Independent Physician Associations (IPAs) and Physician Hospital Organizations (PHOs) that were formed in the late 1980s are not the same as the ones being formed today. Many of those models have dried up and died, or, were rejuvenated by leaner, more integrated, risk-bearing models with sophisticated infrastructure. Still, in my travels throughout America as a speaker/author, I find we still have an overabundance of those old IPAs being formed, operated, and joined for lack of a better model—or is it just plain "apathy," and folks not wanting to bother to change something, take the time and effort to learn a new way to manage managed care, or wait for someone else to take the initiative? Which is it in your case? Only you know in your heart and soul for sure.

IPAs and PHOs have been around for years. Look at some of the older models, Carsle Clinic, in Illinois; Geissinger, in Pennsylvania; Mayo Clinic and Cleveland Clinic, Ochsner, in New Orleans; Harris Methodist in Dallas, et al; Friendly Hills in California; the old Sacramento-Sierra Medical Group known as the "Clinic Without Walls" . . . say those words in Sacramento and duck! Physicians there wrinkle their noses and roll their eyes back when I say those words, because they provoke pain. Pain of the learning curve. I give them credit, though. At least they tried to do something. Better to have tried and failed, than to have not tried and died wondering if . . . !

Rationale

In managed care, we have all witnessed unprecedented change organizationally, competitively, and contractually. We have seen an increase in the development of independent practice associations (IPAs), physician-hospital organizations (PHOs), and management services organizations (MSOs). Many of us have heard at least three subjective uses of the above-mentioned jargon, and been confused by the users' meaning of the terms in their specific case. To quote noted healthcare attorney Alice G. Gosfield, Esq. "If you have seen one (IPA), then you have seen one (IPA)."[1] I believe that this is the case with not only IPAs, but PHOs and MSOs as well. These organizations are seeing their heyday now because of the driving forces outside our world of stethoscopes, scalpels, and sterile fields. The market is demanding the change we see about us, in front of us, and what we have already been through that has come and gone.

There are many reasons to consider the development of these organizations and associations. For the ease of discussion, allow me to call them *products* rather than reciting the alphabet litany each time. I consider them products because it will be easier to subliminally focus your thoughts around the business side of healthcare that is involved in the art of medicine, rather than clinical issues that are so near and dear to your heart. These reasons include positioning for negotiating and contracting leverage, assumption of risk, management of risk across a continuum of care, to secure patient population, including subsidized patients. Another reason we build them is to facilitate existence within the ever tightening cost constraints that are a part of managed care, namely: lower reimbursement, preservation of patient access, maximization of efficiencies, impending risk transfer through capitation and case rates, and dealing with increased overhead and paperwork hassle factors. I will address each one of these individually, but first, I would like to highlight some reasons NOT to develop one of these products.

One reason not to develop one of these products is to think that *by developing the product you will be able to keep reimbursements as they have been.* Simply because you build it does not imply that you will have the power to hold back time, turn back time, or cease and desist the evolutionary changes seen in our

---

[1]Alice writes a wonderful newsletter called *AGG Notes.* Contact her office for further information at 2309 Delancey Place, Phila., PA 19103 (215) 735-2384.

industry. Those forces are even beyond physicians, hospital administrators, and other mortals. I do not know of anyone who has the omnipotence to redirect the flow of market demand for lower costs, premium rollbacks, and increased reporting and accountability. As I listened to Michael (Mickey) Herbert, Chairman of the American Association of Health Plans (AAHP), and Co-CEO and Vice-Chair of Physicians Health Services (PHS), speaking before a group of healthcare professionals at The IPA Association of America's 2nd Annual Conference in New Orleans, I noted many comments about healthcare reform on a worldwide basis. He said that the challenge for both health plans and providers involved with managed health delivery was to "constrain healthcare spending without sacrificing universal access and quality of care." That sentence alone says it all. Things just are not going to be what they used to. Sorry!

Another reason not to build an IPA or PHO makes me want to scream "NO!" from the highest mountaintop! When someone calls my office to ask about my consulting services because they have decided to build one of these networks simply because everyone in town is building one, I want to let the phone ring. My mother used to say, "Are you going to jump off a cliff simply because everyone else is?" (If she were alive, I might have been able to see what she could do for them!) I guess you heard the same line growing up? So then why is it different now? Why build one simply because everyone else is?

Another faux pas I often see is a hospital or physician group developing a product for which there is no market. No managed care nor large population of subsidized patients in the geographical area exists. What is this nonsense? If you build it you will be ready *if* they come? Not even the Boy Scouts motto: *Be Prepared* gets carried this far! The product has to answer a need and a market that will buy. And unlike other marketing techniques, this product cannot create the need if there are no substantial populations of patients or managed-care plans in the region. Size up your market firsthand by incorporating the customer in the design process. If you cannot find a potential customer, you have a problem.

Another warning sign that you should rethink your decision to build might be when your community's healthcare providers are not educated about integration, or are not interested or

willing. In this case, timing might be off and your idea may be pre-
mature. Step back and learn more, teach more, or hire an expert.
I am often called upon as a motivational speaker for hospitals,
groups of physicians, or hospitals and their medical staffs to present the options for developing a product when the leadership individuals are ready but the rest of the staff has not had enough
education or motivating influence (a/k/a "fear") to make them
want to develop a network.

As for organization impact and change, we have seen many
examples and many choices for organizational structure as IPAs,
PHOs, and MSOs. The healthcare publishing market has a
plethora with books on integrated healthcare delivery systems
written by many of my esteemed colleagues. Most have addressed the development of mega-systems such as the Carsle
Clinic, Geissinger, Scripps, Sharp, Friendly Hills, Mayo Clinic,
Cleveland Clinic, Marshfield, etc. There are also writings on
building MSOs that purchase and manage large practices developed by venture capitalists and others. These systems are stel-
lar performers in the integration market on a large scale. Yet,
they are not your typical neighborhood PHO, IPA, or MSO. Hence,
my hope is that this book will address the local, hometown concerns of building a neighborhood PHO, IPA, or MSO by everyday
physicians and healthcare providers that have to survive in
these treacherous times ahead.

The method of competition has changed as well. I am a firm
believer in the spirit of competition. Competition is good for
business. Yet, in order to compete, one must have the right
equipment for the job. In this day and age, in order to compete
for the assignment of and access to patients, physicians, ancillary providers, and hospitals must be positioned properly in the
marketplace in order to be considered worthy of such assignment and access. They do so by competing for market share as
an organization that is designed with the specific marketplace in
mind. Therefore, to simply have membership in an IPA, PHO, or
MSO in your community is not enough. In order to compete (and
win) an organization has to have the right design specifications
and operation, not simply have the members "circle the wagons"
and declare your existence in the marketplace to challenge all
comers.

Strategic planning, marketing expertise, and positioning is required in order to meet the basic criteria to compete in this business. We compete on the basis of quality, service, access, and price but many disagree on how these terms are uniformly defined in measurable terms. Perhaps we should allow the buyers to tell us how they grade the system, and against what values. The term "value purchasing" is an industry buzzword, and has been for the last few years. Yet in a mid-1996 seminar on managed-care marketing in Chicago, I asked a highly-educated audience how many people had heard the phrase or understood its meaning and only three people raised their hands. Value purchasing is what the buyer does when it rates services, quality performance, access to the providers, and pricing using the buyers own relative value scale, and deciding how much of each item they want and how much value they perceive they are receiving for their dollar. Therefore, an understanding of purchaser desires and values is key to effective and successful competition among networks in our industry. Let us not forget that if a group of providers establish an IPA, PHO, or MSO in a neighborhood with the above-mentioned clinics, those mega-clinics will be the competition. The new organization will have to define early on, in the feasibility planning stages, where to highlight the value and place relative emphasis and pricing strategies on niche abilities if that is what the market is looking for, or they may develop an organization that is not able to compete.

Finally, contracting in managed care has changed and keeps changing almost overnight. Rapid actions on the behalf of payors through consolidation, mergers, and acquisitions has changed the *Who's Who* of healthcare payors to "Who are they today?" Or even more important, "Who will they be tomorrow and will I have that contract signed and accepted so that I do not lose my market share and my access to patients?"

Payors have declared that they do not wish to be in the network development business. Think about it: it costs money, time, and lots of effort to build a healthcare network. If they can get you to do it, why would they want to do it for you? As long as the payors' stipulations and guidelines are met with regards to network design and credentials, they get what they want without having to pay for the privilege of hands on development or the hassle factor associated with development. You eager beavers do it for them, and often times forget to negotiate the terms and conditions for having done so, I might add!

Nonetheless, payors now want to contract with integrated groups wherever possible (if the group meets criteria and demonstrates the values that the purchaser is looking for), rather than enduring the expense and time necessary to contract with individuals on a single-provider basis. This would then provide a logical explanation that in markets where the payor has chosen to avoid IPAs, PHOs, or MSOs to contract with when the organizations exist in the community, it must be because the organizations merely exist, but do not fill a buyers' need or do not demonstrate value in the buyers' eyes. I have seen many organizations throughout the country that face this dilemma daily. They built it, but nobody came!

As a participant, you see yourself gathering together with other like-minded individuals to achieve a common goal: mutually beneficial, equitable and fair, successful long-term contracts. Actually, most payors believe they have this goal too, but they have other concerns that they have calculated as business people.

The payor sees you as a network of providers where they can obtain services by negotiating with one centralized point of contact, one voice, one signature, and one file folder. In a medium-sized HMO, a provider contracting representative often makes a salary of about $30–45,000 annually. Now add about 12% for benefits package and about 25% for employment costs and the expense is roughly $52,000. Now divide that by 52 weeks per year, $1000 per week. Then divide that into a 40-hour week, which equates to a cost of about $25/hour, or $0.42 per minute. Meeting time at your location costs time plus mileage at a minimum. Let's say the distance to your office is 14 miles back and forth at $0.31/mile and that parking costs $2.50 per hour. Let's figure that this person and his/her supervisor goes along for the meeting, who makes $35 per hour. The meeting takes 2 hours. The payor calculates the expense of this meeting as roughly $129.34. Do you have one hundred dollars to throw at a meeting? Not hardly! But then, your office administrator costs about $25 per hour, and the prep time for the meeting was about four hours—so you have just spent $150 in preparation and meeting time. Oh but you say you hired a consultant to attend the meeting as well? That can cost you an average of about $200 per hour for an advanced level managed-care consultant. And the surgeon wants to attend at his/her hourly rate of about $175 per hour. All in all, we are estimating a meeting cost for two hours of about $950 or $425 per hour. Now how many physicians are there in the community who have to go through this routine to negotiate or renegotiate their contracts? Let's say that 140 physicians are involved in a meeting of similar length in 50 practices in the area. Not everyone can hire the consultant, so some go it alone. Not everyone hires a professional practice administrator at $25 per hour, but some do. Let's call this meeting time an average of $310 per hour. Get out the trusty calculator folks. The HMO spends $65 per hour and they have more money than you. This represents x% of their net income. Each physician practice spends $310 to get the job done, per hour. The physicians spend a total of $37,200 for each practice to meet with the HMO rep for two hours! Can an IPA negotiate or renegotiate collectively for all 140 physicians in 60 practices for less? Absolutely!

Therefore, the purpose of this book is to provide a basic understanding of the development and operation of the local, hometown integrated delivery system, be it an IPA, an PHO, or an MSO. Since many of the concepts are the same, my approach will be in three stages. The first, design considerations of the IPA and PHO. Then, on to the MSO issues. Finally, an appendix in the back of the book may assist you with some of the documents frequently seen in the development and operation of these three groups. As a consultant in this field, and having built or assisted in the reformation or ongoing operation of about 50 of these organizations, I have seen some excellent projects and some that should never have been attempted.

This book is dedicated to all of you who have tried and succeeded or failed, and to all of you that are thinking about trying to change healthcare for the better. My heart is with you. My prayers include you. We are in this together—physicians, dentists, psychotherapists, nurses of all types, midwives, dietitians, home healthcare agencies, hospital administrators, outpatient and rehabilitation facilities and their administrators and staff, health lawyers, consultants, accountants, actuaries, reinsurance underwriters, physical and occupational therapists, speech therapists, massage therapists, chiropractors, podiatrists, optometrists, and the myriad of other providers that are out there serving us and each other as the continuum of the healthcare industry. We all have a stake in the future of health delivery in America, but we must not give in to the "nay-sayers," the pessimists, the "stick-in-the-mud's," and those who would not bother to try lest someone else figure out how and expend the energy. We must not be afraid of change, but must embrace it. And let's face it . . . I feel better about change when I effected it myself rather then when its designer is unknown to me, do you not?

In closing, let me share something personal with you. There is a wonderful song on an album called *Relationships* (BeBe & CeCe Wynans, Capitol Records, Inc. CDP 77243–8–28216–2–5). It is called *"We Can Make A Difference If We Try."* The lyrics are wonderful and inspirational. One verse in particular makes me want to play the song at every meeting over and over again. Allow me to share with you my favorite verse from the song:

> "All it takes is courage and some time . . .
> If we strive together with one purpose and one mind,
> Let's pray and lift our voices to the sky . . .
> We Can Make a Difference if We Try."

Take the courage and the time . . . we CAN make a difference if we try!

I wish you all the good luck in the world.

Maria K. Todd

1

C H A P T E R

Independent Practice Associations (IPAs)

The time has come for medical providers to think of themselves more in terms of entrepreneurs in search of a place within a continuum of care, niche. Every other industry has turned to niche-marketing . . . why not private healthcare providers of all types?

The era of managed care is well underway and is not going to go away. It is, however, changing at unprecedented speed. What was commonplace six months ago is gone and a new trend has replaced it. Thus, we need to begin to work with the system as it is and where it is going, as accurately as we can determine and make it better for you as professionals, your employees, your patients, your payors, and your community. In response to pressures on the practice of medicine, new practice management styles and organizations need to be created to meet market demands. Managed-care environments have encouraged the development of IPAs, closed panel HMOs, and other corporate structures to provide care for their patients. Early resistance of physicians to joining in administrative arrangements are melting. Providers are beginning to adopt the philosophy of joining resources for survival and to improve market penetration.

Networks are forming as subgroups of other second generation organized IPA forms of practice, in an effort to form third-
generation groups to cope with the eminent change on the hori-
zon, perhaps, some say, moving recklessly into areas of
uncharted growth, or perhaps not moving fast enough depending
on perspective. The Clinton Healthcare Reform Package was like
a train in the distance (the light at the other end of the tunnel?)
and everyone in the tunnel (in the dark) seeing the light, simply
wanting to take cover, and take steps to survive its passage without being able to see where they are going.

American healthcare providers looked at what was coming
in the distance and moved like never before. Many got the idea to
circle the wagons as providers and start building shelters that
they had only heard about; some out of fear, some out of defi-
ance, others out of ignorance, and a few with some good planned
forethought and market sensibilities. Some took the time to become educated about integration and capitation, while still others bought assistance through hired consultants and lawyers to
help them build a model that the consultants or attorneys had
seen elsewhere and engaged their consultants with the responsibility to just build something fast. They scrambled to build a
product for impending managed competition.*

Managed competition was a phrase we used widely during
1993, referring to a system proposed by the Jackson Hole Group
that suggested that the individual employees receive a fixed sum
from their employer and the individual employee chooses the
health plan they prefer. If the plan they chose cost more money
than their employer allowance, they paid the difference. The employee would have the tax incentive to select lower-priced options because they would only be able to deduct the amount of
the lowest cost option. The proposal's proponents believed that
this would encourage individual consumers of healthcare coverage to be more price conscious and they also believed that this
activity would cause healthcare insurers to hold down prices of
their plans to make them more attractive and hence, more competitive in the marketplace. Because insurance under this proposed system was not tied to the employer, employees would
have had portability (not lose coverage) if they changed jobs.
Under this proposed system, there was no provision to set

premiums that appropriately covered the risk of an individual patient or risk-specific population.

This reaction to proposed healthcare reform a la managed competition came with a jolt by the telephone ringing off the wall for assistance, as it did many other consultants involved with managed care. We got calls from multispecialty groups, solo practitioners and others. The cry was "Help us build a Clinic Without Walls!" The first lesson learned was never assume that the client knows what he/she wants until you have done the due diligence of defining the terminology! All I knew about Clinics Without Walls at the time was that a group by the name of Sacramento-Sierra Medical Group had one and some of the constituents were not too happy at the time for whatever reason.

—   Once I asked what kind of a "thing" they wanted to build, I got pretty much the same answers: "We want to build *(1)* something that allows us to preserve our clinical autonomy, *(2)* not become one corporation, and *(3)* have "kind of a *loose affiliation* with one another" that *(4)* can bargain with the payors with some clout. We also want it to be able to *(5)* facilitate sharing of overhead, *(6)* preserve market share, *(7)* enhance camaraderie between the providers, *(8)* take advantage of some economies of scale, *(9)* purchase contracting expertise that we might not be able to afford as individuals, and *(10)* have data to do outcomes." "Okay," says the consultant. "We can do that but it might not be called a Clinic Without Walls, if that is all right with you. How about if we call it an Independent Practice Association or IPA?" This was usually met with, "Call it whatever you want, but can you help us build it, how much will it cost, and how long will it take?" responded the client.

Since then, the above conversation has been repeated nationwide, and amazingly over the years and months since, it remains essentially unchanged. For example, one such encounter with a group in mid-1993 went like this: After meeting with a small group identified as the ringleaders or in more professional terms the "steering committee," and questioning them as to their goals and objectives, we began the actual development of the IPA. Together with their selected corporate attorney, we accomplished some of the initial objectives of starting the group off with its *Articles of Incorporation*, a legal document, normally filed with a state agency that gives the entity birth in the eyes of the law. It basically declares who the parents are, how much influence the parents are legally entitled to, and several other declarations about the entity for everyone to see. The document is then accessible to anyone through the Freedom of Information Act (FOIA).

Next, we ratified the bylaws of the organization to be able to form and empower some committees so that the organization could do some business. This involved designing tasks to be done by committees and forming decision trees. We also assisted with the determination of governance structures. The attorneys provided the group with template documents that were then customized to the needs of the organization.

What happens next is usually based on the level of commitment of the group. If the group wants to move ahead with contracting with payors, they will usually design a credentialing application and a provider services agreement. Most often, the group will engage in some sort of social credentialing, by asking if everyone of the board is in agreement that the prospective member should be allowed membership in the organization unless there are any opposing votes or questionable concerns on the application. A typical IPA provider services agreement and credentialing application can be found in the appendix section at the end of this book.

For the most part, many IPAs had the intentions to follow through with their goals and objectives beyond that point, but many never

* IPA—CHARACTERISTICS

- Separate legal entity which contracts with HMOs and other payors on a capitated basis to provide or arrange for the provision of professional services through independent contracting providers;

- May be shareholder, closely-held entreprenurial model, or broadly held equity model;

- May also perform PPO discounted fee-for-service contracting;

- Except for business flowing through IPA contracts, physicians remain independent contractors; and

- Many anachronistic open-panel, specialty-dominated IPAs being reorganized to empower primary care physicians through equity, governance, and compensation.

really made it. Once they had an organization many went to the negotiation table with the payor and never finalized their quality improvement documents, utilization plans, credentialing policies, etc. They merely existed as localized groups that had been gregariously formed, open to all licensed, interested physicians, whose goal was to retain autonomy, yet have strength in numbers for bargaining power with managed-care contractors—like a symphony orchestra full of soloists! Now, payors having accepted this defense tactic, want a more complete package-including cost effective players, with emphasis placed on financial and quality outcomes.

Second Generation IPAs

Next we began to see the proliferation of the second generation IPA, that meets this criteria and possibly (probably) engages in capitation. These groups are usually a smaller, more quality oriented panel of providers, willing to police their own members . . . a "chamber orchestra" willing to be selected among the best players on an audition basis. As healthcare vendors, you must anticipate the needs of audiences, such as the payors and the patients, and keep your minds open to the possibility and likely reality that these provider-based organizations will form and grow into competitive groups, each with their own niche focus and service style.

Successful implementation of these group practices in the small community require the essentials of availability to patients, consistency of practice, and a friendly hometown approach. The group must have substantial clout with the hospital, specialists, and insuring organizations. The group must have substantial sharing of risk, overhead, and the expense of management skills for the complexities of the business of medicine, which are an essential driving force. The ability of primary and specialty physicians to work together effectively requires a vision of the future and the administrative leadership of the physicians and the hospital administration, with separate, but yet balanced power. Remember, we manage things and lead people!

In many cases, the IPAs in the local neighborhood will grow and partner with other healthcare providers such as hospitals and management-services organizations. A new organization whether an PHO, MSO, or other set of letters must be given birth from some parentage and a local IPA is as good a start as any. However, the group must be well designed with a more homogenous mix, made up of providers with different interests, locations, hospital affiliations (where applicable), and specialties. The common vision to organize an effective single business entity to maximize economic clout, provide quality care, and yet preserve some of the traditional values of autonomy is necessary. Without this "bigger picture," actions fall short of everyone's need. If you cannot satisfy a need, there is no reason for product development. The marketplace has no need for another brand of Widget!

The second generation IPAs have historically been loosely organized, overly dependent of volunteer time, and fragmented by organizing around hospital affiliations or particular insurance plans. Usually, no single IPA can offer everything for you as an individual healthcare provider. You may find yourselves required to join multiple organizations to achieve your goals.

For example, organizations meant to provide advice on contracts could only provide broad concepts rather than getting into the nitty-gritty of negotiation or strong advocacy because of anti-trust concerns that severely weaken any collective process or structure, especially in IPAs.

IPA—ADVANTAGES

- A vehicle for physicians to participate in true managed-care risk contracting;

- Low capital/risk model for physicians to mature into managed care;

- Participating physicians maintain professional and financial autonomy and independent legal status;

- Potential access to sophisticated financial/claims processing/UR-QA systems;

- Depending on provider mix, can produce cost efficiencies and improved utilization profiles;

- Increased leverage in negotiations with hospitals and payors for capitation rates and inpatient risk pool, if the model is appropriate for the market; and

- Advanced IPA models are achieving utilization efficiencies to those of well established integrated group practices.

The potential of a new IPA can be realized by developing a new product for the market. An organization of healthcare providers from different parts of the metro-area, who work with different hospital staffs, and giving the group protection from various shifts and changes of contracts from one hospital to another. This way the group can always provide care, no matter where in the metro-area or what hospital facility. Employers no longer need to be concerned about finding quality physicians in various parts of the metro-area.

The first step in forming this new product (regardless of what you call it: an IPA, an IDS, an PHO, a second generation IPA, a super PPO, etc.) is to abandon the idea that "Doctors do not agree or get together on anything." Perhaps the doctors who do not agree are not mentally ready to change enough to survive in the present and future market-driven and legislated reform. There is no need to convert them, simply move around them. Nowhere is the phrase, "Lead, follow, or get the hell out of the way!" more appropriate. You cannot help those who will not help themselves.

The next step is to grow politically. Economics will follow the politics. Pick leaders who will bring small groups of physicians with them. Gather the "ringleaders" and arrive consensus on the vision, reasons, and needs for the development

IPA—DISADVANTAGES

- May be difficult to create same efficiencies as integrated group practice;

- Difficulties in capital formation; weak systems infrastructure;

- Often unwieldy, specialist-dominated governance;

- Does not affect the expense side of physician practices legal issues;

- Antitrust: may negotiate capitation rates; same antitrust concerns regarding PPO discounted fee-for-service contracting;

- Legal form/corporate practice of medicine: because providing services, must comply with state law regarding form; generally organized as a professional corporation or medical partnership;

- Pension plan issues: care must be taken to avoid aggregation and disqualification of participating physicians' pension plans; and

- Peer review and credentialing issues; malpractice liability.

of the group structure. Never underestimate the power of politically-active leadership-oriented individuals helping to drive the process.

Third, do not wait! Take individuals who are ready and go ahead. Leave the door open for those who want to come later. Do not assume that there is a magic number of individuals required to start the group, or a logical set of specialties. Chances are, if you build something appealing to the marketplace, the providers will bang down the door to get in. Perhaps more providers than you might need or are able to support.

Fourth, select colleagues based upon the general quality of their practice. Do not prejudge; if the practitioners are basically good and committed to the process, invite them in. There is no requirement to take everyone, but on the other hand do not allow personality differences, personal perceptions, or biases to interfere with inviting someone to the group, if only on a provisional basis.

FINANCING AND MANAGING THE IPA

Use an appropriate set of screening mechanisms for the new members to join the group. Obtain all the rudimentary information that is required to join a typical managed-care payor organization. Try to ensure that the members are at least currently economically viable. The reality of withholds and administrative costs during transition must not be financially overburdening.

Maintain existing working relationships and referrals. Do not require referrals within the group as an organizational issue. It may become a problem with Medicare, Medicaid, and other self-referral legislative issues already in place. It comes naturally that the members will want to support their partners, particularly as they develop new practice patterns. Do not damage existing relationships by exclusion. Just keep quality and cost effectiveness when reviewing out-of-network referrals. Be quick to point out recruiting opportunities when outside referral work is well-done and cooperative in nature. It bears repeating that one must remember to plan to remain in conformity with the Medicare/Medicaid anti-kickback restrictions that prohibit remuneration in cash or "in kind" for the value of the referral stream when negotiating with ancillary and hospital affiliates. The OIG Fraud Alert entitled *"Hospital Incentives to Physicians"* will help apprise you of necessary issues for consideration. This issue is addressed at length in Chapter 2.

Construct the business so as to maintain a reasonable degree of management autonomy for the physicians over their immediate staff and facility in which they work.

As far as money management of the basic organization, pay the IPA bills first! No process is more motivating than to realize that the bills get paid first and the members get paid second. It creates a strong, financially sound group with good relationships with the creditors and businesses with whom the group works. Usually, the IPA does not pay its members for anything unless it bills for services under the IPA tax identification number. This is an activity usually reserved for later in the development stage when an MSO is formed or employed.

Do not mess with billing. Unlike the merging existing practices, whereas a new corporation is created and the new corporation would require new provider numbers, new IRS numbers, and even perhaps Medicare numbers by site or facility, depending on the intricacy of the infrastructure, this is not so in the typical IPA. In an IPA, the practices do not merge, but instead retain their corporate autonomy. Therefore, in most cases, joining an IPA does not require that an IPA member start changing numbers or that one must dismantle an exiting billing format within an individual office.

However, there is a need to conform to some centralized or uniform billing practice, as well as a uniform fee schedule. Be advised though, the fee schedule part cannot be done without the proper economic integration and then only with caveats of antitrust laws as applied to the healthcare area. In most cases, the IPA is kept "poor" and maintains "shallow pockets" for the purpose of liability risk management. In this case, it is necessary to keep the economic integration at arms' length by designing an MSO that better meets the objectives of economic integration and thereby addressing pricing, negotiating, and contracting issues at that level. We will discuss that later in this book.

Also, keep in mind that a payor may offer a fee schedule that everyone in the IPA may agree upon without meeting the standards of economic integration. However this does not imply that the IPA has negotiation "clout." It is still not possible for the IPA to propose a set price to the payor so that the payor can access services unless anti-trust guidelines for economic integration have been tested and conformed with. Nor can the IPA collectively disagree with the payors' offers to prevent contracting problems of "naked price fixing" or "boycott." These issues come up when we see a concerted effort to restrict competition in the marketplace arising by the activities of the members or agents of members in an IPA without following the rules about price fixing and boycott, or monopolistic tendencies. Some groups have engaged consultants, who are not experienced and well-versed in anti-trust, to negotiate for them, so as to let the consultant engage in an act of (albeit cerebral) sharing of sensitive information and making suggestions for a group to follow. They might all be playing a few rounds of golf at "Club Fed!"

Do not assume that an IPA needs to create a centralized billing structure overnight. The realization of the need to deal with this issue usually comes about the third month of development. At that point, it is no longer a sales job, but a question of how to achieve co-development of an IPA and an MSO. We will discuss more billing issues in the MSO section later on in this book.

PICKING YOUR CONSULTANTS

Choose a law firm that is familiar with healthcare but that can provide a variety of services. Minimize the learning curve on healthcare issues. This is not a generic business entity similar to a lawnmower sales center. We not only have normal contract law to deal with in this business, but we have so many regulatory overlays that a specialist is needed with expertise developed in this area. In my travels, I have come upon too many generic lawyers who find that a start-up entity is a good opportunity to learn the healthcare area as they go, yet they charge the client on an hours basis, while they spend their time researching and reading what an experienced health law expert already knows. A start-up IPA needs the best expertise its money can buy in the areas of consulting and legal assistance. You either pay in sweat equity and cash or cash and sweat equity!

Make sure that you perform all the due diligence in requesting references, published works in the subject area, and talk to former clients and colleagues. Make sure that you are not engaging a consultant or attorney who only has one solution, one style of project, and one fixed rigid way of seeing the task at hand. Each project is going to have similarities of others but each one is going to have its own design specifications because of differences in participants' cultures, communitized needs, start-up and operating budgets, and educational orientation.

OPERATIONS MANAGEMENT FOR THE IPA

View the corporate office as a service center. Put the patient at the top of the process. If a corporate structure regards itself as the center of authority, as opposed to the center of service, it is not focused on its primary responsibility. The usual task of utilization monitoring and management as well as outcomes, patient satisfaction monitoring and measuring, referral management within the utilization management guidelines, and day to day operations management is best suited for the MSO. However, as an IPA it will be necessary to develop those items to be measured, monitored, marketed, contracted, etc. Then the MSO has something to do!

ADMINISTRATIVE STAFFING FOR THE IPA

Most IPAs do not need large support staff to operate. Many start-ups have operated with a part-time administrative assistant, working as an independent contractor. This person may serve as telephone liaison to the payors, secretarial support to the officers and directors, and may take care of handling IPA mail as it arrives. Once the organization gets larger, a full-time or part-time and full-time person may be needed to assist with credentialing, mailing and faxing of contracts, etc. It may also hire an executive director that answers to the board and carries out day to day business affairs of the organization. The IPA should probably avoid clinical personnel that make clinical decisions or lay hands on patients because of liability concerns. When hiring an executive director or an administrator, do not look only to a candidate with previous experience in contracting, which is the error most often made. Find a candidate with group practice exposure, who is current, innovative, and has a variety of operations management experience; a leader and motivation with a big picture mentality. Find support staff to carry out the myopic details under direct but minimal supervision.

GOVERNANCE ISSUES FOR THE IPA

Governance of the organization is critical. Resist the temptation to slot too many positions and to guarantee the representation of specific interests. Focus instead on the individuals who are elected and expect them to represent the entire group structure and culture. Give the board substantial power so that it can act aggressively on everyone's behalf, yet keep them on a short leash to allow adequate opportunities to replace individuals as necessary.

It does not help an IPA for the members / shareholders to be making every decision; it interferes with efficiency and does nothing to gain the advantages desired in the marketplace.

START-UP CAPITAL

It is going to take time, effort, and seed money to start up an IPA. Be cautious about seeking help from hospitals and other groups that might provide additional early cash. By experience, I have seen groups develop internal cohesiveness if they invest their own time, sweat, and money in the organization. Table 1–1 shows an approximate need for cash seen in many start-up IPAs throughout the country. Please remember that the budget is differentiated from other startup types of integrated delivery systems with other goals and objectives.

It is necessary to look at the table and then rehash what the organization really wants to accomplish in its first year. As a consultant, I would suggest staging the computer system for a later time, and working on one PC for the first year to be able to do word processing, dues, accounting, etc. This would decrease the fax expense, because most department store and electronic store systems come equipped with a fax/modem. I would defer on lots of staff and choose to use a part-time independent contractor secretary, remote voice mail, enhanced fax services from the

TABLE 1–1

IPA Proforma Budget-Startup

Budget Items	Minimum Expense
Legal expenses—documentation filings	$ 1,000.00
Legal expenses—attorneys fees, document prep	$ 10,000.00
Consultant—organizational development	$ 10,000.00
Accountant—counsel, filings, checkwriting, etc.	$ 2,500.00
Commercial artist—logo development	$ 500.00
Wages, commissions (.25 FTE)	$ 5,000.00
Telephone	$ 5,000.00
Postage	$ 500.00
Rent	$ 5,000.00
Office equipment (fax, copier)	$ 7,500.00
Printing	$ 1,500.00
Officers and directors coverage	$ 1,500.00
Errors and omissions coverage	$ (lots!)
Computer system	$100 000.00
Administrative staffing	$ 60,000.00
Misc. expenses	$ 10,000.00
Total:	$220,000.00 estimated through first year

telephone company or other vendor with broadcast fax capability, thus saving lots on postage, office equipment, paper and printing costs, etc. I would also suggest a deferral on errors and omissions coverage until you need it. This is very different from the officers and directors coverage you do want to purchase once you elect the board.

This would make the first year budget pro forma to less than half of the original quote, more feasible, more palatable, and achievable. The way I laid out the pro forma in Table 1-1, I have guesstimated from experience the first year cash projections. Not all of the cash is needed up front. Some of it is needed to begin to develop the organization. Not all the big ticket items are paid in full upon signing a contract with the consultants. Telephone bills need not be hefty unless you plan to advertise with large yellow pages ads from the onset.

Now the next hurdle: where do you get the money? Seed money is necessary at first because you will not be able to sell shares to anyone until the organization is at a stage where it can do so. Therefore, you must rely upon the prospective membership who are not members until they have been credentialed and offered a contract to participate. This means, you may have to develop a means to raise capital. One group I worked with designed a structure so that $850 was initiation fees (non-refundable), $200 was dues for the first year, and at least another $200 was put into an escrow account towards shares when they became available. The initiation fee was accompanied by a pledge of at least 30 hours of sweat equity so that the work was divided among all membership prospects and there was little apathy or blaming. This enabled a group of 140 physicians to raise $88,400 and lots of committee meetings to kick the organization off to a fine start. The additional $200 membership and equity cash was paid upon completion of credentialing and acceptance formally into the group. It also loaded the group with 420 hours of uncompensated developmental time from stakeholders with something to lose in case the apathy mind-set became a problem. The stakeholders were quickly allowed to choose which committee(s) they wanted to participate in, and we gave each committee a rundown of what there was to be done and in what time frame. We estimated the value of their hours at $50/hour. The following committees were necessary to develop the organization.

The Steering Committee

These individuals are the ringleaders who happen to work well together as a team. Hopefully, they have taken time to obtain some education about managed care, integration, contracting, and capitation, have charismatic personalities, leadership skills, and can read marketplace dynamics and activity in the community with an almost innate sense. From this group the officers and directors will emerge.

The Bylaws Committee

This committee is headed by at least one steering committee member that is supported by at least two other prospective members of the IPA to review for current legal and structural conditions. Their actions will set the tone for how the IPA conducts its business affairs and governance issues.

Termination with and without cause may be required and there should be some published policy in the bylaws, if the Provider Services Agreement mentions that such a policy exists. Items to consider include stock transfer, membership rebates on unused portions, return, if any of initiation fees, retention of shares by non-members, etc. A good source of information about termination policies might be gleaned by the IPA from an informational package sold (and available to non-members as well) by the California Medical Association, in Sacramento, CA.

Membership Committee

This group makes suggestions (nominations) for who will be invited to join and what the conditions of membership shall be and communicates this to the bylaws committee for inclusion. The membership committee also designs the Provider Services Agreement to be used as the contract between members and the IPA.

Utilization Management Committee

This committee will perform statistical functions that will set standards and eventually evaluate productivity by Current Procedural Terminology (CPT) code to determine the activities of the group as a whole. This should be headed by at least one board member and supplemented in the physician setting by a team of physicians including specialists, sub-specialists, primary-care and hospital-based physicians. In an IPA of other types of providers, (that is, physical therapists, occupational therapists, and the like) it should have a composite team made up of members with varied expertise. Understand that this committee does not do the day-to-day monitoring, but reviews and makes decisions once the MSO is capturing data and reporting to the Board for review and action. This is why it is necessary to establish only a brief policy statement to begin the organization. So many IPAs mention that member-ship shall abide by the IPAs UM/UR policies in their provider services agreements, yet many organizations who have been in business have them published in the event a diligent member might want to review such a document prior to agreeing to abide by it sight unseen.

The UR Utilization Management Committee will set forth standards and practice protocols or guidelines for more costly procedures and diagnoses to position for per case charges and capitation rates that are inevitable. Among other things, under/over-utilization and adverse selection monitoring, catastrophic case management, C-section rates, hospital utilization, specialty utilization, and emergency utilization must all be monitored by this committee.

Quality Assurance (QA) Committee

This committee will set forth and adopt quality management guidelines and standards, with the power to investigate quality concerns and issues and set forth corrective actions and requirements as may be necessary from time to time. This committee shall also set forth monitoring guidelines to prove implementation and compliance with quality measurement methodologies.

Quality assurance programs in IPAs present a distinct set of opportunities and concerns when compared to group and staff model HMOs. The delivery and reporting systems are complex and diverse. Many managed-care entities are now conforming or adopting as their standard of quality measurement the National Committee for Quality Assurance (NCQA) guidelines. NCQA accredits HMOs only, however, many IPAs and PPOs are adopting the quality measurement guidelines to promote a "me too" attitude. Each system has its own design and thus its own prime objective, with utilization management monitoring tied into the quality assurance program, and based on actuarial data and weighted according to capitation and budgeting philosophies.

Fundamental to any Quality Improvement/Quality Assurance (QI/QA) program is the screening of physicians who participate in the IPA or any other form of alphabetic acronym involved in managed care. Criteria for acceptance beyond provisional status include having proper credentials, accessibility, and quality performance. A medical director, executive director, or administrator must also review the physical location where services will be rendered, the available equipment, and discuss with the provider and staff what will be required for a comfortable relationship with the group.

HealthCare Standards Committee, usually a part of the Quality Improvement Committee or under their oversight as a subcommittee, performs standard setting (non-controversial, measurable and auditable, importance, and potential to show improvement should be the objectives of such a program that this committee oversees). Quality assurance ratings should be determined by medical record audits, member surveys, member transfer rates, and managed care philosophy consensus.

There are many elements of the private practice of medicine that cannot be duplicated in any other setting and which, by their very nature, lead to a high level of physician and patient satisfaction. Intrusions, however necessary, into private physician practices should enhance rather than compromise these assets. Your QA programs should be constructed in a way that lets the physicians test themselves against a system that confirms the value of their individual practices and recognizes individual merit.

Finance Committee

The finance committee sets forth a plan of action for money management, funding, and for the consideration of any non-standard payment mechanisms and carve-outs from capitated arrangements and deviations from established CPT code values. The finance committee will probably also oversee purchasing and capital acquisition matters as well as banking relationships and investment strategies.

Credentialing Committee

This group makes decisions on what the minimum standards of credentialing or the IPA shall be, and hopefully (hint, hint!) keeps its decisions commensurate with both standards set forth for accreditation by the Joint Commission for Accreditation of Healthcare Organizations (JCAHO) and the National Committee for Quality Assurance (NCQA). This group either delegates the task of credentialing to one of the many credentialing houses nationwide, or oversees production of primary source verification as required by the above organizations from an in-house effort. The credentialing committee will also have the responsibility to design a new or adopt an existing credentialing application that will be used for all prospective members to complete prior to actually being accepted as members of the IPA. As for what to request and verify, start with an application that covers the following: name, address, telephone number, home address, home telephone number, DEA registration, board status, malpractice insurance, and proof of licensure which usually looks the same for most physicians. Significant additional data can be obtained by visiting the physician's office and by obtaining both written and verbal recommendations, the latter being more candid. A review of continuing medical education (CME) courses will hint at a commitment to quality care and current level of additional training beyond residency.

Other Concerns Relevant to Pre-qualification for Membership

It is necessary to review the prospective member's office policies and procedures and to establish some basic criteria for membership.

Access Issues

Service locations should be open for a minimum of 20 hours and at least four days per week. After hours coverage must be confirmed in writing, with confidential home telephone numbers and other reach lines of all concerned listed in the cross coverage plan. A review of who provides the after hours coverage is also important. Nonmembers providing cross coverage should be credentialed by the IPA, as many managed-care contracts demand that the responsible party who is contracted warrant and guarantee the performance of anyone performing cross coverage and backup coverage duties. A great deal can be determined about a practice by reviewing the appointment book. A provider with long appointment waiting times or too many visits per hour may infer that he/she is not a good candidate for IPA participation. NCQA has established performance standards with regards to waiting times around scheduled appointments. Most HMOs now try to establish similar waiting time as part of contractual performance. The most popular performance standards I have noticed in recent contracts is right around 15-20 minutes.

Providers should have the capacity to enroll at least 500 new patients. The ability to ensure adequate membership in each provider's office is an important determinant of compliance with the plan's quality assurance plan.

Medical Record Review

The medical records review is significant in several ways. A credentialed Accredited Records Technician (ART) experienced in utilization review and QA should make the first pass inspection, followed by the Medical Director. The review is one of the few times a physician will review records of other providers in their own office; it symbolically indicates that the records of the providers will be reviewed in the future, and it is also an efficient way to determine if the records will pass muster under an audit of the organization's QA system.

Recertification and Recredentialing

The QA committee must recertify offices on a periodic basis. Most do this every two years on a rotating basis, so that the task is not so burdensome. In addition to adherence to the initial criteria, evaluations must cover several categories, with an annual site visit being carried out before submitting a recertification recommendation to the QA committee. The committee may decide to recertify, place on probation, or recommend termination.

Grievance Policies

Grievances should be categorized as administrative and medical. Grievances should not exceed 2:1000 members per year, optimally. It is usually the Quality Assurance/Quality Improvement Committee that develops the grievance policies, although if enough help is available, a separate committee might work a little faster.

Other Operational Issues

Member satisfaction and patient satisfaction are usually relegated to marketing committees, of which there may be up to four subcommittees: provider relations, patient relations, public relations, and hospital relations.

In conclusion, the above overview should help to hone the plan a little more as you begin the arduous task you are about to endeavor. There are many ways under the above topics where assistance from a practice management specialist/consultant would enable you to provide clinical services while receiving help in the developmental stages of the operational planning of the IPA's activities and protocols. The learning curve on the administrative side would otherwise be very costly, rather than retaining an experienced team of consultants. In later chapters, we will review some of the other activities necessary for all groups, whether IPA, PHO, or MSO.

2

CHAPTER

Physician Hospital Organizations (PHOs)

Every hospital is looking to strengthen their physician loyalty bonds by forming Physician Hospital Organizations (PHOs). Increasing competition in the managed care marketplace is forcing both providers and facilities to re-evaluate their alliances and find ways to create a new product to take to market while complying with anti-trust restrictions.

We should begin by first establishing what exactly is meant by the term PHO. A PHO is an organization that unites a specific hospital and its physicians through a contractual relationship. It is usually owned by both the hospital and the physicians, and in many cases throughout the United States is found to be a 501 (c)3, not-for-profit organization. It is an entity that can negotiate with Managed Care Organizations (MCOs) and employers, while allowing physicians and hospitals to coordinate delivery of care through a jointly self-managed system, rather than allowing the payor to manage from the outside looking in.

PHOs are able to offer more enticement to MCOs and employer groups who prefer to contract with a single entity for a full package of health services rather than draw-up and maintain several contracts with various providers individually. The enticement is in the reduction of labor-intensive management, utilization review, and quality assurance tasks. There are still a few managed-care payors that prefer to maintain what I call a "divide and conquer" philosophy in the belief that they can negotiate better (usually unilaterally for the payors!) with individual providers and manage care better (for whom?) than most providers.

Careful consideration must go into the design and management of a PHO to provide premium quality of care and financial and management efficiency. Often times it may be inefficient for a small PHO to manage itself, as there may be goal conflict between the physicians and the hospital, resulting in confusion and anxiety among the participants in the group. Most often these conflicts arise in the areas of financing, revenue allocation, administration style, subcontracts, carve outs, and control.

Initial financing of a PHO is a dilemma. Hospitals usually have more ability to come up with startup capital in much higher amounts than individual physicians. However, in order to have balanced control, the hospital should never be the sole source for financing. Both the physicians and the hospital should have equal risks and incentives, with negotiations keeping vigilant of that objective. Both groups should also share in profit and loss equally in order to conform with antitrust matters.

PHO REVENUE ALLOCATION

Revenue allocation, otherwise known as "who gets what" and "how much" is another hot topic. MCOs like to make capitated/ risk sharing arrangements with PHOs. It makes for easier bookkeeping for the MCO, and makes for grizzly nightmares for the PHO who has not done its homework in cost accounting and actuarial forecasting. It is even worse for the hospital that has just recently launched a marketing campaign to become recognized as the community leader in cancer care, high-risk obstetrics, or cardiac specialty care, without also sending a message that they do great outpatient care. In order for capitation and risk sharing to work, all the players on the team have to be playing the same game with a common philosophy for utilization of resources, including specialty referrals, ancillary services, and technology.

When a PHO is able to attract from a payor, usually it is able to attract from 70 to 80% of premium dollars if it is really prepared to deal. By prepared to deal, I mean not only a hospital, but also physicians, ancillary providers such as home health, DME/HME, respiratory care, pharmacy, lab, radiology, optometry, chiropractic and podiatric services, mental health services, ambulance and air rescue services, trauma and tertiary care arranged, etc. At that point the budget is usually allocated at about 40% to hospital and other services and a professional services budget of about 28% to 32%. The other dollars are usually spent on several things such as reinsurance, plan management, referral management, etc.

PHO DIRECT CONTRACTING

For this reason, many full-fledged PHOs who have already created the MSO component, either within or without the PHO structure, often seek direct contracts with local businesses. This has been seen more in the western United States than anywhere else. I have also seen a lot of this activity in Texas, where for some time the attorney general has been waiting and watching as PHOs engage in activities that might be construed as being in the "business of insurance." For the present time, I have noticed that the message from most insurance commissioners remains "no direct contracts that involve capitation on a direct basis." Why not?

The reason is simple, say a PHO that does not go through the rigors of licensure as an insurance product might take capitation from the direct contract source. What happens if the money has been paid as capitation but for whatever reason the PHO cannot render services as necessary? Who does the payor turn to for remedy? Who pays for the covered services that employees, union members, or whomever needs them from within this direct contracted group uses them? This is especially important when contracting with Employee Retirement Income Security Act (ERISA) (self-funded employer) groups. These groups establish a 501(c)9 trust subject to Department of Labor guidelines, one of which is to maintain a certain threshold of liability per employee which would be transferred at the first dollar of capitation paid to the PHO. Therefore, ERISA plans, in most cases may be prohibited from capitating a PHO directly without working through a licensed insurance company or HMO. They can however, contract direct on a fee-for-service basis. They may even wish to use the MSO as their administrative services organization (ASO), third party administrator (TPA), or employee benefits administrator (EBA) if the services are sufficient, essentially the same, and priced right. Sometimes the user fees that ERISA plans pay to PPOs, TPAs, and the like to access the discounts are upwards of $14 per-employee per-month (maybe even more), depending on the size of the client.

It is possible however, for any payor, ERISA or otherwise to contract directly with a PHO on a fee-for-service basis without going through an established managed-care organization such as an HMO or PPO. We see this activity on the rise as many employer and purchaser coalitions become more and more popular throughout the country.

NEGOTIATION AND PROJECTION HINDRANCES

What hinders the negotiation process in the early days of a PHO for the physician and outpatient is the lack of qualified and verified data from such a variety of players. Since none of the physicians bill as one comparative entity as a whole, it is difficult for the hospital to assess referral patterns and practice styles from a purely statistical point of view. Without knowing peer comparisons adjusted for age, sex, catastrophic cases, and adverse selection it is difficult to massage what little data is available and come up with a rationale for any cost-based system of revenue allocation for both the hospital and the physicians of the PHO.

Further differences can be demonstrated in a system with minimal internal medical management from that with a medical management system designed with a high degree of complexity and the relative discounting acceptable to participating providers. It is difficult to fashion a plan accounting for differences in revenue allocation between providers of similar type as well as types of providers. Everyone must work together to achieve consensus to the intention and methodologies used to calculate the allocation of revenue and then adjust psychologically and professionally any necessary personal changes to work the plan. Communication is key here, with all involved parties receiving and understanding documentation of the methodologies used to calculate the revenue allocation.

DIFFERENCES IN ADMINISTRATIVE STYLE AMONGST MEMBERS

Administration style is a major difference because physicians generally are products of a top-down, uncomplicated (monarchical) management style very different from that of the integrative or management style needed to run a hospital. Both the physicians and the hospital must think along the lines of their historical adversaries, the insurers, as the PHO is essentially a smaller insurance company or MCO. It is often noted that self-administered PHOs might not demonstrate the maximum efficiency if membership is small. Whether the PHO is self-administered through its own Management Services Organization (MSO) or is administrated by an MCO, reporting mechanisms are crucial to regularity and timeliness, and a clear understanding of what is being communicated by the reports to all participants.

Often the reports are fairly periodic (usually monthly) and less than timely (usually delayed by a full quarter) to evaluate services incurred but not reported (IBNR), but are generally so full of percentages, rankings, and gross number calculations that few recipients of these reports can make sense of what it is they are trying to interpret. The educational value of these reports, though well-intended, are many times tossed in a drawer for further review at a later date . . . much later!

If the PHO is self-administered, it must have an experienced management team capable of truly communicating with both the physicians and the hospital administrators and have appropriate data integration systems and report generation abilities. This mix is difficult, as PHOs are newly defined organizations and the need for having an administrator with this unique combination of talents and pioneering vision is not easily found. Most hospital administration programs in accredited universities "churn" hospital administrators-to-be, with little clinical experience necessary to be able to empathize with professional staff. Most of the MCO administrators tend to be graduates of finance programs with little, if any, of the clinical background needed to assess quality and utilization numbers with any sort of epidemiological significance.

Most physicians tell you that if they wanted to be managers and administrators, they would not have gone to medical school.

When it comes to subcontractors, the PHO has the ultimate responsibility; therefore it is critical to establish a budget and manage subcontractors such as psychotherapy, lab, imaging services, and physical medicine in strictest conformity with that budget. Often, MCOs will subcontract through the use of a network capitation model, whereby the subcontractor receives a prospective budget per-member-per-month (PMPM) and all claims received are paid against that pool of funds. Should the funds be more than enough to cover claims incurred, an incentive is received of more monies than the provider billed for each service. Should the services provided overrun the budget, a risk is deducted from the billed amount to offset the deficit. At no time is the established budget tampered with. This instills strong incentive for subcontractors to monitor their own utilization and outcomes for optimum performance under their capitated contract.

Exceptions as to what will be excluded for capitated responsibility are referred to as "carve outs." When negotiating with MCOs, if the PHO is small in size, it may be necessary to negotiate a carve out from the PHO capitation and let the MCO deal with those subcontracted services. This writer feels that if the PHO will be full service, it is wise to obtain the actuarial data and projections, as well as actual historical provider utilization reports and establish a budget for direct subcontracting.

GOVERNANCE ISSUES—CONTROL

Control is probably one of the most hotly debated issues in PHO management. Ideally, the PHO will have equal representation between hospitals and physicians, although the methods for voting and allocating ownership between physicians can vary greatly. Control is a major issue in life, why should it be different in business? All the participants should be satisfied with the representation and the decision process clearly defined and understood to allow for consensus which is binding and as timely as is needed. The law has some regulations about ownership and control.

Governance issues in a PHO are no party because of the myriad of PHO structures that we see throughout the country.

What do you call a PHO that purchases primary-care practices? A PHO. What do you call a PHO that purchases practices and contracts with the former owner/physician as an independent contractor? A PHO. What do you call a PHO that purchases the practices of only retiring physicians and hires new ones as employees? A PHO. What do you call a PHO that purchases the practices and hires the former owner/physicians as salaried employees? A PHO. Like I stated in the IPA chapter, if you have seen one PHO, you have seen one PHO.

So many of the other issues that arise for PHOs are the same for IPAs and I will address them together in later chapters in this book. Such issues as credentialing, membership, and contracting will be covered together as there is little essential difference in the initial development stages.

MEDICARE ANTI-KICKBACK AND PRACTICE ACQUISITIONS

One area that I do want to address specific to PHOs is the Medicare anti-kickback issue related to hospital incentives to physicians. This problem has the potential to arise when a physician becomes employed by a hospital, the hospital purchases the practice, or gives special terms and conditions on loans, services, or office space among other things that could be construed as payment for the inducement of referrals, whether in cash or in kind.

The Office of the Inspector General has become aware of a variety of hospital incentive programs used to compensate physicians either directly or indirectly for referring patients to the hospital. These arrangements are implicated by the Medicare and Medicaid anti-kickback statute, 42 U.S.C. Section 1320a-7b(b). Among other things, the statute penalizes anyone who knowingly or willfully solicits, receives, offers, or pays remuneration in cash or in kind to induce or in return for:

A. Referring an individual to a person for the furnishing or arranging for the furnishing of any item or service payable under the Medicare or Medicaid program, or

B. Purchasing, leasing, ordering, arranging for or recommending purchasing, leasing, or ordering any good, facility, service, or item payable under the Medicare or Medicaid program.

Violators are subject to criminal penalties, or exclusion from participation in the Medicare or Medicaid programs, or both. In 1987, Section 14 of the Medicare and Medicaid Patient and Program Protection Act, (P.L.100–93), directed the Office of the Inspector General of the Department of Health and Human Services to promulgate (develop) "safe harbor" regulations. These "safe harbors" were published on July 29, 1991. (42 C.F.R. sec. 1001.952, 56 Fed. Reg. 35, 952).

In these relationships between physician and hospital, it is necessary to beware of certain activities that may prove suspect of violation including the following:

1. Payment of any sort of incentive by the hospital each time a physician refers a patient to the hospital;
2. Use of free or significantly discounted office space or equipment (in facilities usually located close to the hospital);
3. Provision of free or significantly discounted billing, nursing, or other staff services;
4. Free training for a physician's office staff in areas such as management techniques, CPT coding, and laboratory techniques;
5. Guarantees that provide if the physician's income fails to reach a predetermined level, the hospital will supplement the remainder up to a certain amount (This one has some side rules that come into effect in healthcare manpower shortage areas. Check with an attorney well versed in health law.);
6. Low-interest, interest-free loans, or loans that may be "forgiven" if a physician refers patients (or some number of patients) to the hospital;
7. Payment of the cost of a physicians' travel and expenses for conferences;
8. Payment for a physician's continuing education courses;
9. Coverage on the hospital's group health insurance plans at an inappropriately low cost to the physician; and

10. Payment for services (which may include consultations at the hospital) which require few, if any, substantive duties by the physician, or payment for services in excess of the fair market value of the services rendered.

One document floating around since December 22, 1992, a letter to T. J. Sullivan who was at that time, Technical Assistant at the Office of the Associate Chief Counsel of the Employee Benefits and Exempt Organizations of the Internal Revenue Service, from D. McCarty Thornton, then Associate General Counsel at the Inspector General Division, answers Sullivan's question regarding the IRS's views concerning the application of the above Medicare and Medicaid anti-kickback statute to certain types of situations involving the acquisition of physician practices by hospitals.

Attorney Thornton stated in his response: "We have significant concerns under the anti-kickback statute about the type of physician practice acquisitions described in your inquiry to us. Frequently, hospitals seek to purchase physician practices as a means to retain existing referrals or to attract new referrals of patients to the hospital. Such purchases implicate the anti-kickback because the remuneration paid for the practice can constitute illegal remuneration to induce the referral of business reimbursed by the Medicare or Medicaid programs." He goes on to further state that, "Since tax exempt hospitals are generally required to participate in the Medicare and Medicaid programs as a condition of obtaining or maintaining their tax exempt status, the anti-kickback statute is necessarily a significant issue to be addressed by them."

Further in the letter, he addresses suspicious or troublesome practices that might lead the officials to believe that there is an inducement by the way the deal is structured. He says, "The following are specific aspects of physician practice acquisition or subsequent activities that may implicate or result in violations of the anti-kickback statute. Our comments focus primarily on two broad issue categories: *(1)* the total amount paid for the physician's practice and the nature and type of items for which the physician receives payment; and *(2)* the amount and manner in which the physician is subsequently compensated for providing services to patients." He further addresses the issue of physician compensation in his second footnote that reads, " We would also note that while the anti-kickback statute contains a statutory exemption for payments made to employees by any employer, the exception does not cover any and all such payments. Specifically, the statute exempts only payments to employees which are for "the provision of covered items or services." Accordingly, since referrals do not represent covered items or services, payments to employees which are for the purpose of compensating such employees for the referral of patients would likely not be covered by the employee exemption."

Thornton further elaborates on previous case law decisions in his letter to Sullivan where decisions have been made after scrutiny of the structure of the sale. He states, "Under the anti-kickback statute, either of the previous categories of payment could constitute illegal remuneration. This is because under the anti-kickback statute, the statute is violated if "one purpose" of the payment is to induce referral of future Medicare or Medicaid program business." He addresses the necessity to scrutinize these deals, including the surrounding facts and circumstances to determine the purpose for which payment has been made. He states, "As part of this undertaking, it is necessary to consider the amounts paid for this practice or as compensation to determine whether they reasonably reflect *fair market value* of the practice or the services rendered, in order to determine whether such items in reality constitute remuneration for referrals. Moreover, to the extent that a payment exceeds fair market value of the practice or the value of the services rendered, it can be inferred that the excess amount paid over fair market value is intended as payment for the referral of program-related business." To this point, he quotes a decision statement made in *United States v. Lipkin,* 770 F.2d 1447 (9th Cir. 1985).

To address the issue of the method of the valuation of the practice and fair market value, he says, "When considering the question of fair market value, we would note that the traditional or common methods of economic valuation do not comport with the prescriptions of the anti-kickback statute. Items ordinarily considered in determining the fair market value may be expressly barred by the anti-kickback statute's prohibition against payment for referrals. Merely because another buyer may be willing to pay a particular price is not sufficient to render the price paid to be fair market value. The fact that a buyer in a position to benefit from referrals is willing to pay a particular price may only be a reflection of the value of the referral stream that is likely to result from the purchase. This deviation from the normal economic model was made expressly clear in the safe harbor provisions. For purposes of determining the value of space or equipment rentals, "fair market value" is specifically defined to exclude the "additional value one party . . . would attribute to the property (equipment) as a result of its proximity or convenience to sources of referrals or business otherwise generated." 42 C.F.R. 1001.952(b) and (c), 56 Fed. Reg. 35971–35973, 35985."

The reason that I reiterate so much of this letter is because I continue to see these deals happening throughout the country. The problem is so widespread that more than 500 special agents have been sent into the field from the Fraud Investigation Unit of Health and Human Services, Department of Health Care Financing Administration (HCFA), to uncover, firsthand, the actions, tactics, and strategies of these deals and other potentially fraudulent activities by physicians, hospitals, and others. From talking to and working with physicians involved in PHO activities, I am acutely aware that many either are not aware, or even worse, once I make them aware, their attitude is, "Not my hospital, they would never do anything illegal" or I hear, "It will never trickle down here to this little town." Get real! Fraud is fraud, abuse is abuse, whether you do it in urban America or rural America! Wait there is more!

Thornton points out that, "When attempting to assess the fair market value (as the term is used in the anti-kickback analysis) attributable to a physician's practice, it may be necessary to exclude from consideration any amounts which reflect, facilitate, or otherwise relate to the continuing treatment of the former practice's patients. This would be because any such items only have value with respect to the ongoing flow of business to the practice. It is doubtful whether this value may be paid by a party who could expect to benefit from referrals from that ongoing practice. Such amounts could be considered as payments for referrals. Thus, any amount paid in excess of the fair market value of the hard assets of a physician practice would be open to question. Similarly, in determining the fair market value of services rendered by employee or contract physicians, it may be necessary to exclude from consideration any amounts which reflect or are affected by the expectation or guarantee of a certain volume of business (by either the physician or the hospital). Specific items that we believe would raise a question as to whether payment was being made for the value of the referral stream would include, among other things: *(1)* payment for goodwill; *(2)* payment for the value of the ongoing business unit; *(3)* payments for covenants not to compete; *(4)* payment for exclusive dealing arrangements; *(5)* payment for patient lists; or *(6)* payment for patient records."

Thornton says that any payments for the above are questionable when there is a continuing relationship between seller and buyer, and when the buyer relies on referrals from the seller and that these arrangements raise grave questions of compliance with the anti-kickback statute. I love his closing statement in the letter. He says, `'We believe that many of these arrangements are merely sophisticated disguises to share the profits of business at a hospital with referring physicians, in order to induce the physicians to steer referrals to the hospital." Gee, that was to the point!

In any event, the PHO business has, and will continue to be an interesting strategy for hospitals and physicians and other ancillary providers of healthcare services. Clearly the time for change has arrived. Everybody in healthcare is convinced that the current marketplace is serious about doing something to change the system as it currently exists. What the changes will be are still somewhat of a mystery. All provider types are rushing to position themselves in a posture that will enable them to accommodate the reform as it is mandated.

Following in Tables 2–1 and 2–2 are two outlines that I use often to weave my way through the issues of PHO development, whether in the form of a for-profit or a not-for-profit structure, whether standard PHO or a medical foundation. You may find it helpful as a checklist.

The reason I have not elaborated these items is because many would require a skilled health law attorney to address them appropriately. For me to address these items in detail

T A B L E 2–1

PHO Checklist

Purpose/Description
Legal entity of MDs and hospital
Facilitate contracting
Improve management cost and use
Create new healthcare resource
Legal Structure
For profit
Not-for-profit
Taxable
Tax exempt
By contract
Ownership
100% hospital
50% Hospital, 50% MDs
Governance
Composition of the board
Appointment or election
Decision making
Committees
Management
Part time versus full time
Hiring authority
Reporting relationships
Staff size
Focus of Activity
Managed-care contracting
Direct-employer contracting
Product development
Policy Issues
Authority
Contracting parameters

TABLE 2–1

PHO Checklist—Cont'd.

Policy Issues—Cont'd.

Credentialing decisions
Provider payment decisions
Lock-in of providers
    required to participate in every contract
    "opt-out" choices available
    exclusivity arrangements
Utilization management policies
Quality assurance/quality improvement policies

Financing

Initial capital development
Outgoing expense funding
Hospital capital contributions
Physician capital contributions

Legal Issues

Antitrust
Fraud and abuse
Tax exempt issues
General taxation
Corporate practice of medicine prohibitions in each state
State insurance laws
ERISA
Tort law
Securities law
Errors and omissions coverage
Officers and directors coverage

Legal Documents Necessary

Bylaws, articles of incorporation
Service agreements
Shareholder agreements
Purchaser agreements
Management agreements
Antitrust compliance program
Credentialing application

TABLE 2–1

PHO Checklist—Cont'd.

Legal Documents Necessary—Cont'd.
Credentialing process
Securities disclosure document
Financing documents

TABLE 2–2

Medical Foundation Outline

Purpose/Description
Legal entity focused on the management and delivery of quality healthcare services
Legal Structure
Tax exempt corporation
Ownership
MD Owned
Hospital Affiliated
Governance
Corporation
Decision-making process
Management
Background required
Resources needed
Reporting relationship
Focus of Activity
Practice management
Managed-care contracting
Research
Ancillary services
Purchasing

T A B L E 2–2

Medical Foundation Outline—Cont'd.

Focus of Activity—Cont'd.

Facilities development
Accounting
Billing
Personnel employment

Policy Issues

Practice evaluation
Benefit plans
Authority to contract
Exclusivity
Participation criteria

Financing

Hospital support
Hospital / MD support
MD support
Loans

Legal Issues

Antitrust
Fraud and abuse
Tax exemption
Corporate practice of medicine doctrines
ERISA
Tort law

Legal Documents to be Developed

Membership agreement
Bylaws, articles of incorporation
Employment agreements
Credentialing criteria
Credentialing processes
Financing document

would mean that I was giving counsel without a law degree and license, which could be misconstrued by the reader. Therefore, I will address the issues that I can in later chapters and with some sample documents in the appendices. The intent of the two outlines is to get you thinking along the lines of the task that lies ahead in developing either one of these organizations and to prompt you to seek competent professional legal counsel to get you started in the right direction.

Hospitals that build PHOs from a self-serving standpoint, where they retain unequal control by virtue of their ability to provide financing will have trouble. They may find that as physicians and ancillary providers become more educated to the system, they will have PHOs with a roster, but the loyalty will be with the PHO that provides the balance of power.

To determine if a PHO is appropriate in a specific case requires thorough analysis. The fact that everybody is forming one does not mean that all PHOs can be formed as clones of one another. Hopefully this chapter has provided some insight into the more common issues involved in the formation of a PHO.

3
CHAPTER

Management Services Organizations (MSOs)

Management Services Organizations (MSOs) should have three basic elements as part of their relationship with providers and ancillary providers. First, the MSO provides management services for the providers and other users, as well as access to capital for expansion. This relieves the provider from being distracted from patient care by assuming the day-to-day, centralized management functions of the practice, including capitation, contract management, marketing, utilization management, continuous quality improvement activities, group purchasing, and support services such as transcription, human resources development, billing, collections, and claims management services.

Second, affiliation with a MSO allows reorganization among the group to provide a vehicle for economic integration without blending the practices into one unified corporation, thereby allowing an Independent Practice Association (IPA) or several affiliated IPAs to affiliate with one MSO. Governance, real estate, compensation, and quality improvement issues can be addressed in an organized fashion, preparing the group for its future relationships with capitated managed care and facilitating direct contracting with employer-sponsored healthcare coalitions.

Finally, if desired by the providers, the MSO may purchase certain assets of the medical practices, providing equity of the practice that might otherwise not be liquid to the provider. This activity provides a one-time benefit to the providers in a group that might enable them to realize a return on the value of the on-going business unit that they developed if they left the practice on other terms. This third activity is not a requirement, however, of MSO development.

Often times, we see providers who might not otherwise look for a buyer in times of financial uncertainty such as these, with dwindling profit margins and escalating overhead to gross ratios, look to anyone who will buy the practice as a "bailout" mechanism. These are usually solo practitioners who cannot see a brighter future ahead unless they forge ahead with the "fire sale." They are often exhausted, frightened, frustrated, and have lost the opportunity to see beyond the immediate situation; have waited too long to "partner up" with other solo practitioners and do not see any other way out but to sell the practice to the first entity that will buy.

Faced with the decision to move ahead with MSO affiliation, the providers need to move to the next step of a "make or buy" decision. MSOs come in a variety of arrangements. The best arrangement is for the providers to make their own if they can handle the capitalization. This is usually in excess of $500,000 for start-up and approximately $2 to 4 million for the first year cash requirements. Here the providers have full ownership and re-sponsibility for the success by the management team that an-swers to them directly. The provider-governed Board of Directors makes all final decisions on contracting issues, allocation of rev-enue, and risk and asset management, while the staff carries out the decisions of the Board as provider advocates with no other agendas. Only a fully-owned model can guarantee this advocacy.

Other options include rental of an existing MSO operated by other parties such as management teams, who supply contrac-tual services but offer no equity, or sharing in the development of a MSO with the hospital who may require management control and decreased autonomy in ambulatory care services manage-ment. Often times, hospital administrators who may have never administrated a provider practice, feel that their management expertise and experience in hospital systems management transfers over to management of the day-to-day operations of a small, non-departmentalized business unit. Typical matrix management and top-down management styles, and the teachings of the "three-legged stool" known so well by all health administration/hospital administration M.H.A./M.B.A./M.P.H. candidates do not apply or transfer to medical group administration. Understanding of provider patient-centered concerns, market differences, customs, and values must be taken into consideration when evaluating management style and philosophy. Medical groups cannot be managed successfully as a hospital "department."

Another alternative might be to joint-venture with venture capitalists willing to co-capitalize a MSO with the providers. Experience shows that these individuals have strong ties to bottom line performance and may not be willing to merely be silent partners with a checkbook. The providers values, concerns, and customs, may be sacrificed in this arrangement thwarting the cultural development and socialization that is so vital to the success of the organization. One possibility might be to co-venture with the chosen ancillary providers who may participate in the integrated healthcare delivery continuum, as these small businesses also will be required to participate in the centralized billing, capitation, and sub-capitation carve-outs but may not be able to fund their own MSO venture. Careful planning and development is required in this model so as not to create any regulatory violations concerning Medicare—Medicaid anti-kickback issues and Stark II concerns. The group must seek an experienced health law specialist for this task.

Undertaking due diligence in the evaluation of partnering the development of a MSO is critical to the success of the entity. Time must be taken to make a carefully thought-out decision, as divorce in this situation does not come without great emotional and financial expense.

The medical group must be able to evaluate its current governance structure in order to successfully implement the reorganization of its affairs to allow for coordination of the operations management in the MSO relationship.

Provider independent contractor agreements may need to be revised to allow the MSO to serve as a messenger-model entity for the purpose of contracting with managed-care payors. The governance structure and by-laws of the organization must reflect the intent of how the organization will conduct its business affairs. Careful consideration must be given to the selection of leadership, how providers are credentialed into the group, and "rightsizing" for contracting efficiency addressed. The MSO stands as its own entity and as such must respond in a representative capacity to the medical group. Day-to-day business operations of the medical group performed by the MSO must be addressed in a forum that will contain selected representatives of the medical group in a manner that preserves medical group advocacy.

The role of stock ownership in the medical group should be reexamined and modified to mean that owning stock and voting rights to elect a Board of Directors and Officers, not significant ownership in assets. A Shareholder's Agreement should be prepared to reflect decisions made in this area. Experience has taught us that members should vote their membership democratically and not their shareholdership in a one-person-one-vote system to balance power.

To implement a MSO, the medical group must first begin planning and preparation on the administrative and provider relationship levels. The administrative staff should identify all the contractual and other business relationships that will be assumed by the MSO once the entity is up and running. The medical group will have to contact all lenders, vendors, lessors, and other interested third parties, as may be necessary, early in the process. Obtaining consents from third parties, especially in the area of managed-care contracts is a time-consuming process. Other activities that will be centralized, such as group purchasing, waste disposal, transcription, equipment leases, insurance policies, etc. must all be reviewed. Some third parties will need sufficient notice to review files and process a payoff or assumption request and/or negotiation.

One difficult task is to organize effectively the individual providers to accept the management services concept. The old phrase "If you have seen one MSO, you have seen one MSO" is very true. When speaking of investment in an MSO, most providers will listen to plans about how to diversify revenue and maintain a strong position with managed-care payors. But telling them they have to bill collectively and send all their billings into the MSO sends them into a panic! Regular communication efforts, both formal and informal, must be made to the medical group to foster involvement and support for the project. Meetings with provider staff members are an important aspect of the process. Individual concerns must be addressed, openly and honestly, with the group's leadership being prepared to address all concerned providers on a one-on-one basis.

The leadership of the group should be prepared for the reality that some of the providers will not find the MSO affiliation an acceptable means of doing business. Although every effort must be made to maintain the core group, morale issues may develop if easy exit arrangements are not available for those providers desiring to leave the group. The rapidity of change may be more than some can handle. After all, to date there are no HMOs in Alaska, so they will have some place to carry out their lives and practices in a state of "ostrichosis."

The MSO relationship will require a management agreement that specifies how the MSO relates to the medical group, what services the MSO provides, and the governance mechanism by which a business partnership is created between the medical group and the MSO. Here is where the provider ownership of the MSO is most favorable. Will the MSO serve as contractor and manager of the providers with its own agenda, or will the MSO manage the business dealings of the providers as advocate for the providers with a provider-driven agenda? The MSO should not interfere with the active practice of medicine. The medical group must look to the MSO expertise to provide business advice and coordination of the business aspects of the practice of medicine. Highly-trained, exemplary administrative and clerical employees of the medical group become employees of the MSO, while technical employees will likely remain with the medical group because of federal and state regulatory compliance issues, such as OBRA '93 (Stark II) which requires employees used in ancillary services to remain under the direct supervision of the medical group rather than the MSO. Future anticipated developments in furthering the intentions of OBRA '93 will most likely discourage consolidation of ancillaries at the MSO level. With strong combinations of management expertise and patient-centered quality medical care, the group is destined for success.

4

CHAPTER

Private Practice Management Firms (PPMs)

Private Practice Management Firms (PPMs) are management firms that specialize in the management of large clinics or IPAs on the basis of an ownership, management agreement, or both. You may recognize some of these firms, namely: Phycor, Mullikan/ MedPartners, PhyMatrix, etc. These are the organizations some die-hard individualists love to hate. They are seen my some as the 800-lb gorilla that has come to get their hands in the medical practices of America. But are they really so horrible?

In my humble opinion, I believe that some are good and some . . . well . . . suffice it to say that it depends on what you are looking for in your management and investment goals as to if the decision to participate in some way with these firms is good or bad. (Maybe politics is my next calling?—not hardly!) As recent as 1992, many of these firms were referred to as the "venture-capital sharks" that were lurking just below the surface waiting to see what chum would be served in the "buffet" of failed practices and physicians about to lose their practice and quite possibly their lab coats. (If Harvey McKay had written about the medical industry, the title of his book would have been *"Beware The Naked Physician Who Offers You His Lab Coat."*)

Recently, these PPM firms have been deemed summarily "The new sweethearts of Wall Street." For example, PhyCor is a physician-driven consolidation organization that provides access to capital, management, and systems while touting to preserve a significant autonomy for the physician groups and IPAs that they organize and manage.

PHYCOR

PhyCor believed in 1988 that market forces were beginning to drive a reformation of the delivery of healthcare in the United States. It was founded on a single, focused premise that in order to make significant favorable impact on the cost of healthcare, someone had to work closely with the physicians to produce a vehicle that enables physicians to make the necessary changes to align appropriate business, medical goals, and objectives and respond more positively to the angst of change and respond with a patient centered, medically appropriate vision and a plan.

While this concept did not take rocket scientists to come up with it, it was difficult to implement. At first, PhyCor tried new and innovative ways that might or might not work. It was a trailblazer, with little ability to learn from another's mistakes, because there was virtually no competition in the marketplace. This gave PhyCor precious time to experiment with different methods that would shape the future of what the company has become today as we know it.

When PhyCor went public in 1992, Wall Street did not know how to classify this segment of the healthcare industry, which made valuation of their securities a real challenge to analysts. Analysts were quick to validate the power and concept that were clearly recognized early in 1993, due partially to the intense focus on healthcare reform at the advent of the first Clinton administration. With that recognition came the advent of the competition in the PPM segment of the healthcare industry. At the same time, a similar project was developing at the ancillary provider level with names like NovaCare, Rehability, and HealthSouth.

As of April 1997, PhyCor had 47 affiliated clinics, 3280 physicians and 53% of those were primary-care physicians. The serviced patients and managed-care plans in 500 service sites, including 17 IPA markets with 930 physicians were involved in that subsegment of the business. They operated in 60 markets, including 23 metropolitan markets, 30 regional, and 7 rural markets. They managed 2.1 million managed-care lives of which 880,000 were capitated Commercial and Medicare lives.

Often PhyCor is seen as a catalyst to accelerating the formation of organized delivery systems in the marketplace. Droves of independent physicians are choosing to join with PhyCor through the affiliated organization rather than continuing to practice independently or joining with a competing organization. In 1995, about 90 physicians, representing about 50% growth for that year's physician participant roster. joined through practice mergers when their groups affiliated with PhyCor. Of which, about 80% of the 1995 growth was in primary-care physicians, furthering the company's goals of expanding its primary-care component.

PhyCor attributes its growth in its physician organizations to physician leadership who can communicate a vision that attracts others to the fold. They also differentiate themselves from other competitors in the way that they focus on the qualitative and quantitative attributes of the company that keeps it consistent in its track record of growth, expansion, and operational innovation and flexibility.

PhyCor states that their mission has been clearly stated since the formation of the company: *"To create, with physicians, the best value in medical care for our communities."* Their company values include the idea to *"Do what is right–respond to needs–care for people–be the standard–and project pride."* Their guiding principles at PhyCor include the following:

- Provide the business, management, and capital resources that enable physician organizations to best serve the needs of their patients;
- Commit the company to physician organizations that are contributing to value in medical care;
- Create a relationship between medicine and business that will establish the standards for medical care delivery;

- Develop an organization that will enhance the security and satisfaction of physicians in the practice of medicine;
- Attain a leadership position in the delivery of medical care services; and
- Produce tangible benefits for physicians, employees, investors, and especially patients.

A diagram of the PhyCor organization is shown in the following illustration:

PhyCor Practice Management Company

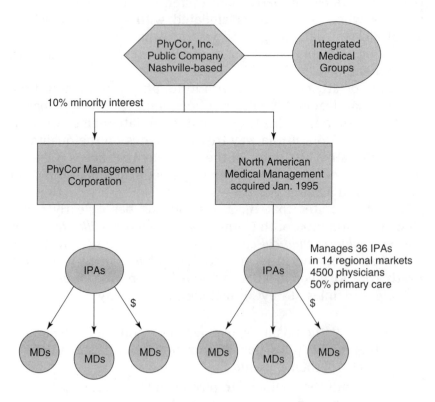

PHYMATRIX

PhyMatrix is a fully integrated PPM that has four components: first and foremost, they are a PPM company. Secondly, they develop disease management networks that focus on disease representing the major portion of the $1 trillion spent on healthcare annually. Thirdly, they are a provider of specialty services that are synergistic to the core organization and lastly, they develop medical facilities such as medical office buildings, medical malls, and health parks. PhyMatrix claims to be primarily a physician practice management company. However, Abraham D. Gosman, Chairman and CEO is not one to leave all his eggs in one basket. A creative mind with a creative leadership team behind him, Gosman has built a service continuum in markets where others dare not enter, namely metropolitan New York, Connecticut, and New Jersey. The company's major presence is focused in the Northeastern United States where they have affiliated with approximately 1425 physicians through IPAs, with more than 600 in New York's five boroughs, 375 in Connecticut, and 450 in New Jersey. In October 1996, PhyMatrix agreed to an exclusive arrangement with North Shore Health System of Manhasset, New York to jointly develop, own, and operate medical facilities in five metropolitan New York counties.

Later in April 1997, they signed a letter of intent with Beth Israel Health Care System to form an MSO to provide management services to the medical community in the greater metropolitan New York area. They plan to acquire and manage the physician practice management operations of Beth Israel Health Care System, which consists of 130 physicians with more than 20 primary and specialty medical offices located throughout New York City, Rockland, and Westchester counties.

The company's strategies remind me of the famous line from Star Trek, ". . . To boldly go where no man has gone before." New York, New Jersey, and Connecticut are such "clique-ish" markets and it takes an insider like Gosman to get in and function within it.

Recently PhyMatrix signed a letter of intent with Tenet South Florida HealthSystem to become the anchor at the PhyMatrix

Medical Mall at Palm Beach Gardens, Florida. This joint-venture will bring Tenet's clinical and management expertise together with PhyMatrix's vision to provide a wide range of outpatient services in a sophisticated environment created with quality care and patient convenience in mind. From the beginning, PhyMatrix's chairman, Abraham D. Gosman, has stated that he wanted the company to embrace a concept of a "bedless hospital" medical mall. Therefore, unlike PhyCor, this company has its own vision that is not quite the same as PhyCor, yet has some comparative conceptual similarities.

PhyMatrix's performance is not too shabby either. They have increased revenue from $2 million in 1994 to $185 million in fiscal 1997. PhyMatrix is active in the following medical support services: radiation therapy, diagnostic services, infusion therapy, lithotripsy, home healthcare, and rehabilitation, and a medical real estate development subsidiary, DASCO Companies. DASCO is the nation's leading developer of medical offices and outpatient facilities and specializes in the development of many types of healthcare facilities, cancer treatment centers, ambulatory surgery centers, medical malls, health parks, medical office buildings, diagnostic imaging centers, and other specialty centers. Its top ranking in *Modern Healthcare*'s annual Construction and Design Survey over the last several years attests to DASCO's leadership position. By integrating the various components of their service matrix, they position PhyMatrix to effectively compete in the market-driven healthcare continuum of the next millennium. Managed care growth has been projected to reach a 50% penetration by the year 2005, will, by definition, be the primary contributor the other growth of PPMs such as PhyMatrix, MedPartners, and the like.

An example of PhyMatrix's organizational structure on page 61.

The PPM/physician relationship provides significant advantages to medical groups that are evaluating strategic positions and preparing for competition. After all, you have the choice of either having the entire managing team of physicians in the IPA or MSO executive board all go back to school and earn their MBA or MHA degrees, or you have to strategically partner with one of

PhyMatrix Corporate Structure
Integrated Networks

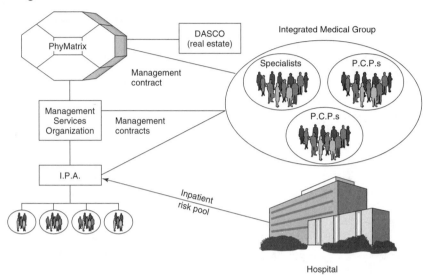

these companies. It is the "make or buy decision" all organizations must face: Do we develop, merge, partner, or acquire the management expertise necessary to compete in today's healthcare market? The answer about PPM partnerships and M&A activity is different dependent on the long-term goals and objectives of each respondent.

In summary, these PPMs such as PhyCor, et al. treat healthcare as a business with medicine as the "art form." And it seems like unaligned physicians are taking a new look at companies such as Phycor, PhyMatrix, and MedPartners who can demonstrate leadership.

Payor organizations also look to these organizations because of their ability to deliver cost-effective healthcare while achieving superior outcomes both clinically and in patient satisfaction consistency. Thus the manner in which IPAs, PHOs, and individual providers can organize themselves, the degree of empowerment they possess, and their ability to set the tone for medical delivery is paramount to their competitive managed-care strategy.

5
CHAPTER

Corporate Form: A Myriad of Choices

Where to begin? When faced with the decision to do something, the first activity necessary is to select and organize a steering or investigative committee that will act as the temporary board and incorporators of the entity.

This chapter will address the organization of the steering committee, their tasks and areas of consideration. Although it is not exhaustive, it will cite the more crucial areas that the team faces in getting the organization off the ground.

ORGANIZING THE STEERING COMMITTEE

Steering committees should have several members, each with different expertise or interests. I will address several types below, including the multi-specialty IPA or PHO, the single-specialty IPA or PHO, and non-physician IPA.

The Multi-Specialty IPA or PHO

This design, being the largest and most diverse team, should be madeup from different factions of the medical staff if you plan to have an all-inclusive, successful, risk-bearing organization. Whether you are designing a multi-specialty IPA or PHO, this committee should be madeup of primary care, specialty, and perhaps even a sub-category of hospital-based physicians. The needs in each category are very different. The team I have found most successful in the design of an IPA steering committee is to have one of each of the following: family practice, pediatrics, OB/Gyn, general internal medicine, gerontology, orthopedics, cardiology, rheumatology or physiatry, general surgery, gastroenterology, diabetology or endocrinology, neurology, and psychiatry, as well as radiology, pathology, emergency medicine, and anesthesia. If I have a team such as this, I can build a Med-Surg IPA, a Medicare product, a Medicaid product, a Workers' Compensation product, and a product to service motor vehicle and casualty insurance products for both PPOs or exclusive provider organizations. This way my organization will stand ready to service all lines of insurance and third-party payors available in the marketplace. I also have a well-rounded team that complements one another in clinical areas. If I can find the members of the staff with the qualities and specialties to make it happen, my steering committee has seventeen dedicated people that will need to serve on at least one subcommittee.

Some consultants might argue that this group is too large to get any work done but I disagree. I look for special qualities in a steering committee, specifically: leadership and communication skills, knowledge of the marketplace, a basic understanding of capitation, and a respect for risk rather than fear of it, a competitive spirit, and an acceptance that this product is needed and desired by both the community and the physicians in the community. I also make sure that each has a good sense of fair politics or charisma to persuade others to roll up their sleeves and join into the work party as needed, and most of all, a genuine interest to take control of medicine and put it back in the hands of physicians where it belongs. Oh, and one more thing: a sense of humor! If all these qualities are present, they are educated as to what the job entails and they come to meetings to be productive, rather than to sit and commiserate. The team I try to develop for this position is too busy to waste time commiserating! Steering committee meetings should have an agenda and stick to it. Parliamentary procedure is a must, therefore, a pro-tem board should be nominated and those not elected as officers should be members at-large. This group should be prepared by a consultant team of an experienced healthcare organizational development consultant, an CPA familiar with capitation, an experienced health law or transactional law attorney, and a healthcare actuary. From time to time I like to add a few members of the business community to lend their ideas to the group.

The Single-Specialty IPA or PHO

In my opinion, unless you have some very specialized niche, single-specialty groups are not for every market, except for certain specialties that deliver services based on a rider inclusion for those services to be covered by contract, such as chiropractic care, podiatry, optometry, or for special services that may be either esoteric or specialized high-cost services that might sustain themselves more easily through a capitated carve-out from a generalized medical loss ration budget. These teams include perhaps, hospital-based subspecialties such as neonatal or perinatal intensivists, mental health and substance abuse services, anesthesia, radiology, pathology, emergency medicine, or other specialties such as high-risk obstetrics, or limited practice groups that specialize in a particular area of medicine as consultants with a short-term relationship to the patient, and no real ongoing follow-up once the crises are over, as is seen in the routine practice of office-based medicine.

It has been my experience that many managed-care plans would rather spend the time and effort contracting with an entire continuum of care rather than one specialty focus group, if given a choice. The reason being that the yield for the time spent is greater with the full-service group. Now that is not to say that there is no validity in single-specialty groups, but that one might experience a more difficult time of it when attempting to attract the attention of a payor entity that is focused on building a network quickly and inexpensively.

In working with a group of orthopedic surgeons who wanted to build an orthopedic IPA only, we realized quickly that in order to monitor utilization, control costs, and quality concurrently,

the physicians would have to hand pick a team of support players. For instance, who was going to put the patient under general
anesthesia or manage monitored anesthesia control (MAC) while
they operated? Who would carry out physical therapy orders?
Who would dispense prescription medications to their patients?
Who would manage any medical comorbidities?

In a capitated carve-out situation for orthopedics, in order
to gain more clout and control more of the premium dollar, they
would have to subcontract with all these players on the cursory
list above. This is something to consider as you develop your
goals and objectives for development of your group, because the
management of the entire continuum of services related to orthopedic cases is not only the way to gain data and truly control
utilization, but it is also a value-added service to the payor that
centralizes the groups activities rather than providing still another fragmented piece of the delivery continuum. Payors like
that and are usually willing to transfer dollars and delegated responsibilities to the group well developed for that intent.

The Management Services Organization (MSO)

The steering committee for the MSO has a similar task to the IPA
and PHO in its development, with the exception that it has to
have leadership at the helm and an ability to speak at many levels of understanding. These people are the linguistic translators.
They can speak medicalese, legalese, accountingese, actuari-
alese, insurance-ese, and computerese, and they can communicate to the rest of us and tell us what they want the organization
to do for them through departmental development and delegation of responsibilities. Most often, the steering committee for
this group sets out to steal a contracting expert from a local
managed-care organization thinking that this person will be the
"Messiah" and will *handle everything* from the moment that they
are hired. NOT!

The first thing that the MSO steering committee must do is
decide upon the activities and role that the MSO will play in the
management of the clinical team that is related at arm's length,
and may be the same investors in a different organization with a
different corporate set-up.

When the steering committees begin their due diligence and strategic planning, one of the first steps it must take is to decide upon a corporate form. Some of the more popular and possible appropriate forms the corporation may take (whether an IPA, PHO, or MSO) are: general partnerships, limited partnerships, regular or C corporations, Subchapter S corporations, and the most popular (and the new darling of the bunch) the limited liability corporation. In the following pages we will compare those listed above. Naturally, it is imperative that you seek appropriate professional competent counsel for your specific needs. The comparisons set forth are very general as this book is intended for a readership from a variety of locations and corporate intents.

General Partnerships

A general partnership is a voluntary association of two or more individuals for business entities who agree to work together for a common business purpose. The partners, who own the business, share their profits or losses equally or as otherwise provided by agreement. Like proprietorships, partnerships can be formed easily. No formal steps are required to establish or maintain a partnership. In order to confirm certain aspects of their relationship, many partners enter into a written partnership agreement to specify their understanding (a meeting of the minds) on matters such as, how the profits and losses of the business should be allocated, procedures for admission of new partners (stock purchase/entry documents), and withdrawal of existing ones (exit arrangements documents).

Partnerships offer business owners "pass-through" tax treatment. The partnership does not pay income tax. Instead, the income, profits, losses, and expenses of the partnership flow directly through to the partners, who report their allocable share of income and expenses on their personal tax returns. Because partnership income is not taxed at the partnership level, operating a business as a partnership is, like a proprietorship, attractive from a tax perspective.

Disadvantages of General Partnerships

Personal Liability   Liability is the biggest problem with partnerships. **In a general partnership, each partner is personally**

liable for all debts and obligations of the business. The consequences of this rule in a worst case scenario could prove disastrous. If one partner innocently (or negligently) makes a mistake, it could cost all the partners. The problem is especially significant because individual partners may be forced to satisfy the business obligation out of their personal assets if the business assets are inadequate.

What About When Someone Leaves the Partnership? A big problem with partnerships is that they lack business continuity. Without an agreement to the contrary, whenever an existing partner ceases to be a partner, whether as a result of retirement, death, expulsion, or the like, the partnership ordinarily is deemed to have been dissolved as a matter of law. Steps could be taken to continue the business, with or without one of the successors or heirs, if any, but the process is not automatic. If the heirs or successors decide not to continue the business, they could require a distribution of partnership assets and force a liquidation of the business. Talk about job security for attorneys and accountants! Given the volatile emotions and personalities in our healthcare delivery force, this is probably not the best way to go for a large group of corporately unrelated and related physicians in the form of an IPA or PHO, and it certainly would spell expensive doom for a true MSO of independent participants.

Lack of Investment Flexibility General partnerships are financed either through capital contributions made by partners or by the use of debt. Most often in physician groups, the capital call is through personal funds. Rarely have I seen phsycian groups begin with a loan signed by the partners because they just do not start out a group endeavor like this with outside debt. Hence, many of these initiatives are sadly undercapitalized. I believe more than anything else, unless they have an MBA, they have not had the training and experience in business endeavors to know their options, nor do they each have the time or the inclination to approach their banker for money for a start-up that has no business plan, no corporate form (yet), no strategic market assessment (yet), or a good way to verbalize what the *group's* vision of the organization will be (yet). Although there is some flexibility to finance a general partnership, it is often less than that available in other business forms because a decision to bring in a new partner to raise needed money usually requires allocating some management responsibility to that partner.

Advantages of Limited Partnerships

Another form of business is the limited partnership, which is a distinct legal entity created under state law. Every limited partnership has at least one general partner who manages the limited partnership, and at least one limited partner. Limited partnerships, by contrast, can raise money from limited partners without conferring management responsibility as well. Therefore, limited partners have very little say in managing the corporation. In exchange for their limited control over partnership affairs, the limited partners have limited liability for partnership obligations. They are at risk only to the extent of their investment in the partnership. The general partner, by contrast, has unlimited liability for the partnership's debts and obligations. A limited partnership is formed by filing a certificate of limited partnership with the designated state agency, typically the secretary of state. The partners can structure their relationships with each other and address certain business issues through a limited partnership agreement. Anyone who is aware of the NAMM-IPAs in the Houston market that were created in 1993 through North American Medical Management were formed as limited partnerships with one gentleman at the helm, who now works with PhyCor.

Pass Through Tax Treatment   Although the tax treatment of limited partnerships is extremely complicated, if appropriate steps are taken, the income and losses of the business will, like those of proprietorships and general partnerships, flow through to the individual partners in accordance with their partnership shares via a K-1 document, filed with each investors tax return. This structure avoids the double level of tax caused by a tax on the business itself.

Financial Flexibility   Limited partnerships offer more financing opportunities than general partnerships because the former provide a vehicle for raising money (from limited partners) without

having to take in the investors as general partners. In some instances, financing techniques are simpler to implement than
those techniques available to corporations.

Limited Liability of Limited Partners   In a limited partnership, a limited partner, whether a person or a business entity, is personally
at risk for the obligations of the business only up to the amount
invested in the partnership. The party's liability has been limited
and personal assets cannot be used to satisfy the obligations of
the business. In exchange for this limited liability protection,
however, a limited partner is given a minimal voice in managing
the partnership's affairs. A limited partner who participates in
the management of the business in a more meaningful way will be
stripped of this limited liability.

Disadvantages of Limited Partnerships
General Partner Liability for Business Debts   Unlike limited partners,
the general partner in a limited partnership is fully liable for the
obligations of the business. In order to insulate themselves from
unlimited personal liability for the debts and obligations of the
business, many individuals who manage a limited partnership
will establish a corporation, retain sole ownership of that corporation and have the corporation (which must be adequately capitalized) serve as the general partner. This machination may insulate an individual's personal assets from claims by creditors of
the limited partnership, but it is expensive, cumbersome and
adds additional layers of complexity to the business management process because naturally each layer adds legal fees and
more documentation. Just what every healthcare practitioner in
America needs (only kidding)!

Another principal disadvantage of the limited partnership
form is that it precludes a segment of its owners each limited
partner from participating in the management of the business.
Although most states provide some "safe harbor" rules specifying those management decisions that limited partners are free to
participate in, unanticipated or ambiguous issues are bound to
arise, and such rules offer little guidance. The penalty for a limited partner whose participation in management affairs exceeds
designated limits? The limited partner loses its limited liability

protection and has personal exposure for the obligations of the business. As a result of this draconian penalty, a limited partner may feel helpless watching the general partner make decision after decision that hurts the business and the limited partner's investment. The prospect of such helplessness often deters prospective investors from committing their capital to a limited partnership.

I once worked with a vascular imaging laboratory that created several limited partnerships for the purpose of purchasing a Multigon Duplex Imaging unit that cost around $49,500 to purchase. The man in charge of the operation ran a telemarketing unit to solicit limited partnership units, contributing a minimum of about $5000 (or more) to the endeavor. He closed the capitalization of each limited partnership at $130,000 to cover operating and marketing expenses. Then we had two talented gentlemen who "placed" the equipment into physician offices and trained their medical assistants or nurses to perform limited studies on patients meeting medical criteria for the examination by history or symptoms. Suddenly, Medicare, who was the primary payor for this type of exam changed the billing and eligibility criteria to use the equipment and the endeavor was no longer profitable. When the general partners made the decision to fold the partnerships and liquidate the equipment, the investors were very angry and helpless. They could do nothing more than watch as their investment slipped away, the company folded, and the general partners went on to their next endeavors. The payroll and expenses for the general partners were lavish, the scene unbeknownst to me was a repeat of what had happened at another similar corporation that was in trouble with the Securities Exchange Commission (SEC) for similar questionable activity.

Once the company folded, I received a house call from the SEC, inviting (translation: intimidating and compelling) me to come down and have an informal chat (with a court reporter in attendance and a tape recorder in motion) with a couple of guys (with badges and guns) and to bring all software, notes, and papers in my possession to the little "chat session." I knew very little of what they wanted because I was sequestered from the activity of the telemarketing and its related paperwork and activities and was only involved in the business and compliance issues on the clinical operations related to the use of the equipment. It left a bitter memory of what can go wrong with limited partnerships and general partners actions. Add the volatility of healthcare reimbursement rules and technical equipment issues and you have a potential for success or a potential for disaster.

Advantages of Corporations

The corporate form is now considered the leading business form in the United States. If you remember back to your history classes from high school, Americans saw opportunity during the industrial revolution, where adventurous businessmen and women searched for a way to invest capital without risking their entire personal resources. These risk takers also required a business form that would not require liquidating the business because one or more investors wanted to leave the business. Corporations offered the perfect solution. Regular (or C) corporations, as they are called, are formed upon filing a certificate of incorporation with the secretary of state or other designated official in the state where the business is to be established. Once established, corporations are recognized by law as distinct legal entities and have the power to act in their own name as persons. Corporations are owned by shareholders, but managed by directors and, upon delegation of authority from directors, by officers as well. These officers and directors carry liability in their decision-making and must act in good faith and in a fiduciary manner so as to protect the investors in the same manner and fashion as the other investors in the corporation. Therefore, they need to be insured in the event that their actions are cited in a liability action by one of the shareholders, members, or anyone for that matter. Corporations provide their owners with a number of very attractive features. To name a few, limited personal liability for corporate shareholders/owners as long as certain criteria are preserved, continuity and transferability of debt or equity interests to other interested parties.

Limited Liability for Business Owners Corporations are treated by law as separate and distinct entities from their owners. As such, their liabilities are generally treated as separate and distinct from those of their shareholders. Consequently, shareholders of a corporation can generally feel secure that creditors of the corporation will not pursue them to satisfy claims. Also, shareholders are protected from claims by an individual sustaining personal injuries as a result of an action by an employee of the corporation or caused by one of the corporation's products.

Piercing the Corporate Veil   Notwithstanding the generally recognized concept of limited liability, important exceptions have developed over the years that permit the "veil of protection" a corporation provides to its shareholders to be pierced so that the shareholders may be personally liable for certain corporate obligations. Although a detailed discussion of this doctrine is beyond the scope of this book, shareholders may be personally liable if:

1. They have ignored the formalities required by corporate law, instead treating the business as their alter ego, (an example of which would be writing business checks for personal expenses of the shareholders);
2. A shareholder's personal negligence caused personal injury; or
3. The corporation is insufficiently capitalized to carry out its operations and the shareholder(s) should have expected its under-capitalization to detrimentally affect a party doing business with the corporation. This is one area in which physicians and other healthcare providers who are unfamiliar with business on a more formal corporate level can run afoul of the systems as officers and directors, because they are held to the standards of the reasonably prudent, trained business person. Since they do not have the training in finance and corporate operations on this level, they stand at risk as an officer or director.

Notwithstanding these exceptional circumstances, when carefully planned, the personal liability can be limited for the shareholders of a corporation.

State law endows corporations with an indefinite and continuous life. Every document that I have ever seen as a paralegal for many states indicate this very fact on the Articles of Incorporation. This characteristic is attractive to an individual who, investing capital in a business, would not like the business wound up and dissolved on the unilateral decision by another investor to withdraw capital in the business or, by the heirs in the case of the death of a shareholder. While other business forms can be structured to achieve a measure of continuity, the formality of the corporation does it best. Large corporations survive long beyond the lives and business participation of their initial shareholders and employees. The institutionalization of a corporation can provide significant competitive, financial, and other advantages over businesses that lack such continuity.

Another bonus of corporate participation is that it provides an inexpensive and relatively expeditious means to transfer ownership interests in their business. When there is no agreement between shareholders to the contrary (as may be found in some bylaws), shares of stock in a corporation are generally freely transferable. Indeed, shares of publicly owned corporations like Columbia, PhyCor, and Pacificare are routinely traded on stock exchanges through a phone call to a licensed broker. The convenience of transferability permits investors to move in and out of ownership positions in corporations with lightning speed if their investment philosophy or business circumstances change. By contrast, partners can generally not assign or transfer their interests in a partnership to another party without the consent of other partners. When I overlay the personality types that are involved in our healthcare delivery systems, I have seen some long-standing feuds that would make partnership agreements for a huge IPA, PHO, or MSO endeavor untenable. The high degree of liquidity is an important advantage of the corporation over other business forms, such as a partnership, where it may be difficult or impossible for a partner to conveniently retrieve money invested in the business.

Another corporate advantage that we see in regular or C corporations is that they offer virtually unlimited flexibility in structuring the management of a business as a result of the distinction made under corporate law between owners (shareholders), managers (directors), and day-to-day operators (officers). Common and preferred stock, preferred and subordinated debt, voting and nonvoting stock, high or low quorum requirements at directors meetings, and veto rights for shareholders and/or directors are oniy a few of the many tools that owners of corporations can use to customize ownership and management rights and responsibilities through the wordsmithing of its bylaws.

Disadvantages of Corporations

Because corporations are treated as separate and distinct legal entities, they are also treated as separate and distinct taxpayers. Thus, the IRS and most state governments impose a tax on the income earned by a corporation, which must generally file its own tax return and pay its own tax based on its earnings. When the corporation distributes its income or assets to shareholders, another tax is imposed on the shareholders (either an income tax if the distribution takes the form of dividends or a capital gains tax if the distribution results from the sale or disposition of stock). As a result, income earned by a corporation is taxed twice. Despite limited exceptions where the double tax is not a material disadvantage to the shareholders of a corporation, such as the use of crafty income-splitting strategies (which are beyond the scope of this book), the second tax often raises the cost to business owners operating as a corporation. (It sounds so complex! I chuckle when I imagine what it would have been like for Joseph and Mary to have had to discuss tax strategies like this on their way to Bethlehem! But alas, that was then and this is now.)

The Subchapter S Corporation

The Internal Revenue Code provides a limited solution to the double level of tax problem, it permits certain corporations to elect to be treated in accordance with the provisions of Subchapter S of the code. Unlike C corporations, "S corps" generally do not pay a corporate level tax on their earnings. Instead, all of an S corporation's earnings flow through to its shareholders who, like proprietors and partners, pay a single level of tax on the income of their business. I have this type of corporation for my consulting firm and back in the early days, many IPAs I formed chose this form as their structure because of its simplicity.

The pass-through tax treatment of an S corporation is a viable solution to the double taxation problem. S corporations are not the best choice these days for most IPAs, PHOs, or other networks. The IRS has established specific criteria that limit the eligibility of corporations to elect S status. These limitations are discussed below.

Disadvantages of S Corporations

The most significant disadvantage associated with the S corporation form is that the IRS has limited its eligibility to corporations that meet the following four criteria:

1. The corporation must have no more than 75 shareholders.
2. All shareholders of the corporation must be United States' citizens, resident individuals, estates, or certain defined trusts (corporations, partnerships, and many types of trusts cannot be shareholders).
3. The corporation may not have more than one class of shareholders.
4. The corporation may not have more than a 79% interest in any subsidiary corporations.

Any one of these limitations could easily present a problem to many businesses. Moreover, shareholders who initially meet the requirements for electing S status must continue to meet those requirements for as long as this status is desired. Even an inadvertent breach of the qualification rules can lead to termination of S corporation status. For example, if a new business is being capitalized by investors with different investment objectives, it might be desirable to issue two or more classes of stock (for example, common stock and preferred stock). Such is the case in many IPAs developed by primary care physicians, where they want capital and participation from specialists, but as nonvoting members of the corporation. This decision would preclude S status. Similarly, a physician or other healthcare provider owned business that is founded by 10 participants may elect S status at the commencement of operations but, after the membership drive and credentialing, the number of physicians or other healthcare provider shareholders may easily exceed 75 and so require termination of S status.

Aside from the difficulty of qualifying for S corporation status, the S election also can have adverse tax consequences notwithstanding its pass-through tax treatment. Some of these more important adverse consequences, including limits on the use of debt to create tax basis and the prohibition on the use of special allocation of corporate income must be addressed by appropriately trained, competent professional counsel taking into account your unique circumstances. Make sure the counsel is qualified. I learned this lesson the hard way when my business was audited and a start-up capital transfer from my personal funds was put on the books as cash and I was taxed with interest and penalties by the IRS and the State of Colorado. The accountant that gave me guidance stated that everybody did it that way and the IRS's response sounded like my mother . . . (you know, the old "If everybody jumped off the bridge would you jump too?"). They stuck to their position and I paid . . . lots! CPAs are just like other professionals and craftsmen, some good, some not as good. Caveat Emptor!

Double Taxation Considerations

One alternative for businesses that may not qualify for S corporation status yet seek the advantages of incorporation (limited liability, transferability of interests, management flexibility, etc.) by maneuvering around the double taxation issues.

Income earned by regular corporations is taxed twice, first, on the business entity level and, later, its shareholders are taxed again on the distributions they receive from the corporation. If, however, the corporation has no income, it pays no tax. Therefore, sophisticated entrepreneurs often operate their corporations in a manner designed to limit (not maximize!) income. This is especially true in the IPA or PHO environment where medicine is being practiced and the corporation should be kept (in my humble opinion) cash poor to thwart any attempts at searching for deep pockets and finding them at the IPA/PHO level. Here, one would want to keep the deep pockets at the MSO level and not have any clinical activity going on at the MSO level whatsoever. The shareholders' maneuvering to limit corporate income, yet put as much money in their pockets as possible, must be carried out carefully and delicately. When the corporation can justifiably pay all of its income out in the form of tax-deductible compensation to its employees and operating expenses, the business has no income left to pay tax on. Another common means to limit (or even eliminate) corporate income is to finance the business with debt provided by shareholders. The corporation's payment of interest on the debt is also deductible and the repayment of the loan principal amount is tax free. This compares favorably with the distribution of equity to the same shareholders, which could be subject to a capital gains or ordinary income tax. This is where many goof in the start-up of S corporations. GET GOOD ADVICE from your tax advisor.

Attorneys and accountants often seek additional loopholes to avoid the double level of tax imposed on income earned by corporations. Remember you can avoid paying taxes, you just cannot evade them. Many of these techniques are useful but there are limits to such creativity, and the IRS acts to close such loopholes by constantly developing and refining its volumes of *Commerce Clearing House* directories of restrictions. As a result, even with superb tax planning, most successful corporations ultimately pay a corporate-level income tax, which can be substantial. Many businesses grudgingly find themselves paying the additional tax as the price for the benefits of operating in corporate form. If your long-term goal is to keep the clinical model poor and put the cash in the MSO, get good counsel familiar with healthcare issues and the organizations. Call the Healthcare Financial Management Association (1-800-252-HFMA) for referrals and further information. They can help. And by the way, have one of the steering committee members join the organization for access to superb educational programs and a jam-packed informational membership journal. The membership fees are returned tenfold by the organizational benefits.

The Limited Liability Corporation (LLC)
The LLC offers the following tax incentives and for this reason has been most popularly chosen over the other available forms for IPA/PHO of development throughout the nation, namely:

- Limited liability (to protect its owners from becoming personally liable for the debts of the business);
- Pass-through taxation (to avoid the double taxation attributable to regular corporations), no restrictions on permitted owners (to eliminate the burdensome numerical and other requirements established for S corporations);

- No restrictions on active participation (to ensure that, unlike limited partnerships, all owners could be active in managing the business without jeopardizing their limited liability protection); and
- Operational flexibility (to let owners structure the management in a way that satisfies the concerns and requirements for each business).

At the time of my research, Massachusetts, Hawaii, and Vermont had no LLC options, all other states and the District of Columbia had provisions for them and the start-up filing fees ranged from a low $35 in New Hampshire to a high $500 in Illinois.

As a consultant and a paralegal, I carry a directory of the statutory cites with me when I go out on client sites to work with startup groups and usually can download the actual statutes from a source such as LEXIS. This enables the client to read through the statutes so that they can ask intelligent questions of their attorney, accountant, and of their consultants. In selecting any professional consultant expertise, these things should be made available to you so that you do not have to spend the time searching on your own. You pay us to shorten the research and learning curve. For those of you reading this book, however, if interested, you may call my office and my administrative assistant will have the actual state by state citations for you to obtain by calling your government document depository or your public librarian. Call us at (303) 750-3524 from 9:00 to 4:30 mountain time. We also have a pamphlet available that highlights Limited Liability Corporations entitled *Making the Decision—Why an LLC?* that we mail as a courtesy to present and prospective clients in our information pack for those considering this unique corporate formation. Feel free to call and request one if you are interested.

Other Concerns of the Steering Committee

So far we have discussed the different constituencies and corporate forms available to provider networks. What else does the steering committee have to do? Lets talk a little about strategic planning and business plan development. It is likely that the steering committee will have had the most in educational opportunity and time for consideration, as well as more time to develop leadership and communication skills than the other late comers for the development of your network. Therefore, while the steering committee may or may not become the executive board, it may well become the business development committee by default. This is especially true in smaller groups. The following is a checklist that I use when meeting with steering committees to give some structure and an agenda to the meeting. Although most have capital, they are by no means in a position to waste time or money unnecessarily with a consultant with minimal experience and a "we will both learn it as we go along (since I am billing you for my time)" attitude. I have been called to do cleanup detail on some botched jobs on those who carry briefcases and business cards where some unsuspecting client will become their "n = 1" network project. I now know how some surgeons feel in the surgical suite. Professional decorum makes you keep your mouth shut and do your best. I want this book to be your personal "fishing manual." I am of the philosophy that if I teach you to fish here, you can eat for a lifetime on your own skills and only use consultants for that which you cannot do for yourself, or that which you need to shorten your learning curve to save time and money with a private lesson.

Steering Committee Tasklist

Background/Understanding of Task
Develop a Statement of the Committee's Purpose **For example:** Twenty urologists associated with this single-specialty IPA would like to move forward and develop an independent provider organization for single-signature managed-care contracting in cooperation with their affiliated hospitals and ancillary providers.

As more fully identified below, the scope and purpose of this project is to design and assist in the development of a Provider Organization (PO) and a Management Services Organization (MSO), to assist the physicians and other healthcare providers affiliated with the group in and around the Metropolitan Statistical Area (MSA) of Dupage County Illinois and the Greater Chicagoland area so as to prepare for the demands of managed care.

To the extent legally permissible in accordance with the applicable regulatory constraints; the design of the PO will provide the physicians involved and committed to the project the opportunity to bid and hopefully participate in managed-care arrangements while maintaining a completely independent practice. Each physician or group practice shall continue to bear the responsibility for the cost of all assets, equipment, and supplies of their existing practices. The physicians shall not be relieved of any management and administrative responsibilities associated with their respective practices, except as may be required by then existing regulatory requirements.

It is understood by both the physicians and consultants that the PO shall be designed to provide a structure for facilitating cooperation among the independent individual practices for the purpose of providing high-quality, cost-effective orthopedic care in a managed-care setting. The role of the PO shall be as an Independent Practice Association (IPA) and it shall assist those affiliated physicians with opportunities to develop new and unique healthcare products, while facilitating a sharing of the financial risks and responsibilities associated with the same. To this end, the PO shall develop and provide a consortium of orthopedic surgeons for centralized utilization management (UM), quality improvement (QI) and credentialing, and data collection services for the entire network of providers. The PO generally is not intended to, however, become involved in the day-to-day operations, business risks, management, or ownership of any of the individual practices that are part of the PO, except as may be required by then existing regulatory requirements. This is not to prohibit a change of vision for the future which may eventually combine the practices into one corporation, if desired by the parties.

At first, the PO will provide a structure by which providers may be assisted and supported with the development of managed-care arrangements. Eventually, the design shall be enhanced so that the PO is sufficiently integrated with all affiliated practices so as to take on financial risks associated with capitation arrangements.

Long-range plans include the development of a second organization commonly referred to as a Management Services Organization (MSO) which if developed, shall be designed and developed to provide all the support and management services associated with the PO. The MSO shall provide expertise in centralized management of the business aspects of all the practices in the PO. The MSO may assist with hiring all personnel, provide a mechanism for group purchasing, contracting, marketing, data integration, performing utilization and quality monitoring, billing and collection services among other functions such that the group may desire, all to the extent legally permissible by then applicable regulatory requirements.

Approach   Together with a professional consultant (as needed) with expertise in the management and development of such networks, the steering committee then needs to work on the following tasks:

1. Development of shared vision;
2. Organizational development of the IPA;
3. Organizational development of the MSO;
4. Market focus; and
5. Business plan.

Each phase should conclude with a go/no-go decision, and a deliverable. These deliverables should be spelled out for the consultant by the steering committee so that you can gauge the effectiveness of the consultant and the expenditure of the capital dollars when reporting progress to other interested parties.

Development of the Shared Vision   The purpose of the work session would be to develop a clear statement of goals:

- Develop a clear understanding of single signature contracting;
- Develop a consensus on managed-care direction;
    1. Right-sized network. (This takes market research that the committee may delegate to a marketing

subcommittee or may purchase information from a company such as Sachs in Chicago.)

2. All or selected providers participate (steering committee decides what will be logistically feasible to get the work done).

3. Capitation goals and objectives need to be visualized and strategized.

- Identification of physician interests in leadership to serve the group as developmental leader for the following tasks:

    1. Creation and monitoring of bylaws;
    2. Credentialing and membership;
    3. Utilization management;
    4. Quality improvement—standards of care;
    5. Medical directorship;
    6. Marketing;
    7. Risk management;
    8. Finance and budget;
    9. Business development;
    10. Information systems;

- Develop a statement of target market intent.

Often the consultant assists the team to design, refine, and then document the vision. When we work the project as the consultant, I have found that working with each physician leader to outline work tasks to be completed by the physicians and the consultants together works the best. This way the work is not overwhelming to anyone unfamiliar with the design and development tasks. From time to time the steering committee may need to be augmented by temporary assistance from outside sources on an independent contractor basis for secretarial tasks, mailing, and telephone calls to pull projects together.

From the outcomes of these activities, the steering committee and the consultants usually develop statements of objectives, vision, and mission. This statement is then returned to the shareholders for review before final ratification by the membership.

Organizational Development of the IPA

The steering committee must next either delegate the following tasks or carry them out themselves:

1. Select an experienced, health law attorney;
2. Select an accountant familiar with healthcare and capitation issues;
3. Organize and schedule a meeting of interested fellow participants who will become the general membership participants in an organizational goals workshop;
4. Create lists of all the IPAs, PHOs, PPOs, and HMOs in which participating physicians are members; and
5. Create a list of available resources for utilization review and quality control.

Because the business plan will involve sharing of sensitive market data that might border on antitrust activity, the steering committee must look to the selected attorney for guidance to develop the organizational papers that permit business planning and work the leadership team through the major decisions.

Additionally the committee must also look to the attorney for compliance with all then current regulatory issues and limitations set forth by Stark I and II, antitrust, fraud and abuse laws, and regulations for the chosen organizational structure, and both to the attorney and accountant for consideration of any IRS and tax status implications, and for the requirement of any local regulatory concerns.

Next, the committee needs to design and direct work tasks to achieve the following:

1. Develop a statement of purpose to help the participants agree on goals and objectives of the organization. The proposal may, of course, include goals that will not be immediately realized;
2. Prioritize activities that the PO will pursue and determine how the PO shall operate. The scope of the services dependent on the defined goals and objectives of the organization;

3. Develop a business plan for both initial and subsequent operations of the organization. I have found inexpensive software that is both healthcare designed and user friendly through Biz Plan Builder Interactive from Jian; and

4. Develop the level of understanding of the different task committee leaders.

Next the steering committee needs to work together with the selected consultant team to develop initial documents necessary to form the organization, including:

Articles of incorporation or organization;
By-laws;
Shareholder aagreements;
Participating physician agreements;
Participating payor agreements;
Participating hospital agreements;
Participating ancillary agreements;
Utilization management policy documents;
Quality assurance/improvement policy documents;
Credentialing criteria and procedure;
Grievance procedures; and
Reporting requirements and their schedules.

As a consultant having done many of these, I can tell you that I have completed these documents on a rough draft basis ready for attorney review together with several IPA/PHO steering committees and executive boards over the years and it is now down to a science. Most of these documents should be semi-prepared by your consultant team and you should not be paying for document development from the blank paper stage. Most of these can be accomplished for around $30,000 in consulting assistance, plus respective filing fees, as applicable. If you are speaking to a consultant or an attorney who has never developed these documents before and has to charge you to start from scratch, keep looking. We are few and far between, but we are out here.

Organizational Development of the MSO

Required of the steering committee:

1. Selection of the health law attorney;
2. Selection of the healthcare accountant familiar with capitation and physician reimbursement;
3. Development of an SEC memorandum for investment by other members if the capitalization will be over 1 million dollars; and
4. Participants' decision of physical location of business office.

Because the business plan of the MSO will involve sharing of sensitive market data that might border on antitrust activity, the team must look to the selected attorney for guidance to develop the organizational papers that permit business planning and work the leadership team through the major decisions:

User fees—revenue allocation;

Departmental objectives;

Equity decisions;

Selection of staff and equipment;

Ancillary contracts; and

Ancillary equity participation.

In no event should the steering committee proceed with the development of any business plan based upon any shared market data of the members unless and until clearly identified safeguards can be established to the satisfaction of the group or its legal counsel. With the members on a single-signature corporation with common bottom lines and the intention of a single-signature capitated contracting, it should be possible with appropriate legal guidance to pool market information with less restriction and risk by the formation of an economically integrated MSO.

Market Focus

These steps come next on the steering committee's list:

1. Provide hospital partnership goal, if applicable;

2. Provide capacity of each geographical area for new and converted business;
3. Provide managed-care contracting parameters (if and when attorney states that this is acceptable);
4. Provide current managed-care activity by volume of claims and dollar value; and
5. Facilitate request to physician offices for collection of claims data for outcomes measurement in accordance with HEDIS guidelines.

The objective of the market data research are:

A. Define the breadth of geographic coverage intended in the contracting effort;
B. Identify the competition;
C. Identify market sensitivity; and
D. Identify needed market services.

Development of a Business Plan

Building on the previous phases, the necessary consultants would work closely with the steering committee to build business strategy into a formal written business plan that includes the following components.

Description of the business;
Description of the products;
Description of the market;
Market niche;
Market size;
Description of coverage;
Marketing strategy;
Financial strategy;
Administrative/management structure;
Quality improvement/monitoring of outcomes;
Resource requirements; and
Time line for development and implementation.

6
CHAPTER

Credentialing Issues and Guidelines

When a Managed Care Organization (MCO) allows prospective members into the fold, it must perform diligent credentialing to attempt to ensure that the providers should be expected to provide good quality care. This means that a process by which the participants are allowed to perform within the scope of their training is evaluated thoroughly by those granting the privilege to do so, with whom that clinician shall be affiliated. This process examines licensure, training, professional work history, qualifications, and even the malpractice claims history of the applicant.

Long-standing case law supports requirements that organizations that grant privileges to clinicians go beyond mere affirmations. One such case was the Nork case, which held the hospital liable for the actions of a staff physician because the hospital failed to verify the statements made on the physician's application, and simply relied on his truthfulness. Hospitals are not the only ones being challenged now for this, but so are IPAs, PHOs, and MSOs that grant privileges to treat patients of the network, as well as the HMOs and PPOs that contract with them. This opinion in the Nork case led to changes in the Joint

Commission on Accreditation of Healthcare Organizations (JCAHO) standards that require that no clinical privileges be granted without prior verification of credentials. Other groups such as the Accreditation Association for Ambulatory Care call for review of training and peer review based on education, training and experience, and current competence of practitioners. Similarly, the National Committee for Quality Assurance (NCQA) has guidelines for credentialing within HMOs that a contracted IPA, PHO, or MSO would have to follow as well.

A program of credentialing/recredentialing, whereby credentials should be reviewed every two years based on their original effective date with the IPA, should be developed. When it comes time to recredential (usually one or two years after acceptance into the IPA) recredentialing information should be requested by certified mail, return receipt requested. Note that even where rigorous credentialing exists, there are no guarantees of protection from liability arising from the negligent acts of a participating clinician.

In developing a credentialing policy, it would be helpful to incorporate a two-part policy, containing a mechanism to review and categorize privileges to perform specific procedures and also to investigate whether a specific provider has demonstrated the necessary clinical competence to perform the procedures.

Some of the problems that can undermine a credentialing policy and can actually create liability are failure to verify gathered information, failure to delineate privileges, and failure to follow-up on data gathered.

Many groups perform what I call "social credentialing." A task that involves one or two people reading the responses on an application of someone well known to them professionally. After all, they send patients there on referrals, eat lunch with them, golf with them, etc. What's to examine?

Many groups newly formed, resist the need to establish well-planned and implemented credentialing policies that could prove legitimately defensible in the selection and retention process because they fear it will be too confrontational, and that they do not want to burden the clinician requesting privileges. They prefer to engage in social credentialing, and whether they are aware an applicant has active privileges at the participating plan hospital.

This is similar to purchasing a pig-in-a-poke in some cases. Applicant provided references are also problematic in that colleagues do not usually say much more than "I have worked with him for so many years and feel he would be a great asset to our group." Many attorneys feel that this is downright f\prima facie evidence of negligence on the part of the MCO and that such requests for recommendations should come from the entity and be returned directly to the entity.

Another problem in credentialing often encountered is failure to follow-up on data gathered. Should the entity granting privileges find something questionable in its data gathering, the courts usually consider this as a warning notice to the entity. The failure to act on the information could be construed as entity negligence. This is usually referred to as *nonfeasance*, a failure to act when there is a duty to act.

DUE DILIGENCE IN CREDENTIALING

A good selection and retention program within any managed-care organization should follow certain procedural guidelines, as there are numerous laws that impose responsibility upon those groups or entities that allow medical providers to "lay hands on" patients when the credentialing activities fall short of the necessary due diligence. These are usually addressed under tort or negligence law.

Some of the terms used in this area of law include: vicarious liability, respondeat superior, and ostensible agency. All of these theories of law are predicated on the fact that there is a network established and the fact that there should have been control exercised by one party over another party or the proximate cause of the selection of the individual to the injury. In other words, "If you had not chosen him/her to be in the network, he would not have been there to hurt me."

Traditional negligence law requires that the individual who harms a patient is responsible for his/her actions when the harm is caused by breach of duty of care owed by the clinician to the victim. Why should a managed-care organization that establishes the panel of providers be responsible for that clinician's actions? Three basic theories of law play a big role in the answer to the above: vicarious liability, ostensible agency theory, and master servant or *respondeat superior* liability.

Vicarious liability

Under the concept of vicarious liability, the managed-care organization is liable for a provider's actions because of the special relationship that exists between them, even if the one on whom the vicarious liability is imposed is essentially blameless for the immediate harm. An example of this would be when a managed-care participating and credentialed physician requests time off and has another physician, who is nonparticipating and therefore not credentialed by the managed-care organization, to provide backup coverage for him/her. In the event that the backup physician injures the patient, the vacationing physician may also be held liable because he/she allowed this physician to provide backup services when the backup may not have been qualified to do so. To this end, the MSO may also be held liable because they permitted the backup coverage by a nonparticipating, noncredentialed physician to see the patient, and therefore, the MCO can be found liable for the actions of the participating physician who selected and retained the backup. A lawyer might argue that the MCO should have exercised more control over the participating physician by requiring that only other participating physicians may provide backup coverage to the managed-care patients. Therefore, both the vacationing physician and the MCO would be held vicariously liable for the backup's negligence. To dig a little deeper, the HMO or PPO that allowed the IPA to be the contracted providers, of which the vacationing physician is a member, might also be held responsible because of their lack of control over the IPA, who in turn should have exercised control over the vacationing physician, who should have been required to select a participating physician. This may be one of the reasons why we see some of the "hold harmless" provisions in managed-care contracts. Tort liability lawyers are simply doing their jobs when they dig for the deepest pockets in situations like these. A good credentialing procedure and related policies can help prevent these situations as long as they are not paper policies only. They have to be enforced equally and fairly on everybody on a regular basis in order to be helpful.

Master-Servant Responsibility

Master-servant liability is commonly referred to by its Latin term *respondeat superior*, which is used to describe the responsibilities of the master (employer) for the servant (employee). In managed-care relationships, most often you will see contractual language to attempt to reflect that no master-servant relationship exists, no employer-employee relationship exists. I am aware of several cases throughout the country where this clause in the contract has been tested. The argument routinely used is that the physician or other participant is following policies, procedures, and standards of care set forth by the organization, must be available for work 24 hours per day, 365 days per year, and that monies are paid by a fee schedule and therefore, this is not a clear independent contractor relationship. Often MCOs of all types will include independent contractor language in all contracts, whether IPA, PHO, MSO, HMO, or PPO, so that the payor does not have to deduct FICA, FUTA, and withholding taxes, or pay workers' compensation when tendering payment for services rendered. The courts have, in the past, tested the merits of the case by the facts and not just the written words. In recent cases, they have found the MCO liable as master for the actions of a member. I am not suggesting that you change the participation agreements, but understand that you are not protected just because the agreement says you are supposed to be. For more information, review the Darling vs. Charleston Community Memorial Hospital (33 Ill. 2d 326, 211 N.E. 2d 253 (1965), cert denied, 383 US 946 (1966).)

Ostensible Agency

When the MCO is liable for the actions of its participating providers (and nonparticipating providers who have been allowed to see patients for whatever reason) the law imposes liability on the MCO for the actions of its members who are apparently acting for the MCO, and therefore are presumed to be under the MCO's control.

To explain this further we need to understand the difference between an HMO or other health plan and an indemnity insurance plan. In the indemnity plan, you pay your premium and receive a contract or certificate that declares what is covered and what is not. There is no limitation as to where you may seek care, because the care is unregulated by the indemnity carrier. As long as a physician states that something is medically necessary and it falls within policy limitations and guidelines, the bill is paid at the contract rate. There is no "management of care," no provider panel, and no incentive to use a particular provider network.

By contrast, in an HMO or PPO setting, there is a panel because the mechanism is not that of *insurance*, but that of a *health plan*. In a health plan, the insurance mechanism of dealing with financial risk for the cost of claims is married to a delivery mechanism, and the benefactors of the plan are required to use the specific network in order to maximize benefits through the plan. Therefore, it would stand to reason that those benefactors would be entitled to some protection in the event of being injured by the negligent actions performed by any member of the designated panel of providers that they are required to use.

Some of the traditional credentialing requirements should include the following:

- Physician licensure;
- Board certification;
- Professional liability coverage;
- Professional history and references; and
- Hospital affiliations.

The IPA should also access information from the National Practitioners' Data Bank (if applicable) or other department of professional regulation queries, and take into consideration patient satisfaction surveys, quality assurance concerns, cost utilization profiles, PCP change profiles (if applicable), and the individual provider's commitment to the managed-care team philosophy. In addition, the credentialing committee should take into consideration the provider's open/closed status of the ability to add new patients, chart review scores, ER utilization (if applicable), sanction history, coding practices, cost rankings, and C-section rates (if applicable).

The credentialing procedure can raise problems of its own with regards to conspiracy theories, defamation, civil rights violations, and possible antitrust actions regarding restraint of trade. You should know that the Health Care Quality Improvement Act of 1986 (P.L.99-160) has provisions of law which provide some protections, especially with regards to antitrust concerns. These protections are granted as long as when the MCO prefers an adverse decision against an applicant, the decisions can be demonstrated to be both *(a)* based on firm belief that the applicant would have posed a quality problem and *(b)* that they offered the applicant an opportunity for due process. Another stipulation is that the conditions that caused the applicant to be denied are, in certain instances, reported to the National Practitioner Data Bank.

Any MCO that enters into affiliated relationships with physicians, where the physician has applied for clinical privileges or appointment, is granted access to the databank. Data available includes licensure actions, malpractice claims and settlements, and privilege and membership restrictions by other reporting agencies. In addition, reportable decisions are described as those which adversely affect the privileges of a practitioner for longer than 30 days, including reducing, restricting, suspending, revoking, or initially denying privileges. Failure to report vitiates the protections provided by the Act.

Structuring a Good Credentialing Policy

Begin with a clear and concise statement of policy existence of a process whereby credentials are reviewed and verified through primary source verification, this is mandatory for affiliation with the MCO. State the recredentialing policy and the time element involved as well.

Next, develop the written policy that defines what will be required for information submitted for review. Also, make sure to include some policy on due process for those denied privileges, right to attorney representation, if desired, and how denials will be communicated to the applicant. In addition, spell out how confidentiality will be maintained.

Develop specific form letters to be used, a standard application, and reference request form letters to be used. Attach and incorporate them into the organization's credentialing policy as exhibits.

Finally, stick to your policies and procedures. No matter how time consuming, it is no defense to say the organization was too busy to carry out the necessary due diligence in matters of privileging and retention in a managed-care organization of any type.

In the next few pages, I have listed some of the elements most commonly found in credentialing applications. You may want to use this listing to create a multi-page application for privileges and membership for your MCO. Remember to state in boldface type at the top of the document your design: "This application is for credentialing purposes only. It is not intended to guarantee contracted provider status or membership in the GreatCare IPA (or PHO or MSO)."

You may wish to title your document "Provider Application for Credentialing." I always like to include the following instructions:

1. Please provide ALL requested information.
2. Please type or print.
3. Use "N/A", throughout this application for "not applicable."
4. Attach a copy of your Curriculum Vitae and any other required materials requested.
5. Sign any releases for information.

Sign this application, and return all materials in the enclosed envelope.

General Information:
1. Full name.
2. Federal tax identification number(s).
3. Federal narcotics registration number(s) (if applicable).
4. Social security number.
5. Medicare provider identification number, UPIN number.
6. Current office, principle address, phone, fax, answering service.

7. Alternative office, address, phone, fax, answering service.

8. Home address and telephone number, fax.

9. Date of birth; birthplace.

10. Medical or professional school, attendance dates from/to, degree conferred.

11. If applicable, ECFMG number, FMG Clinical Clerkship location, dates from/to.

12. Internship, location, type, dates from/to.

13. Internship, location, type, dates from/to (if more than one).

14. Residencies, location, address, from/to, specialty.

15. Fellowships, location, address, from/to, specialty.

16. Teaching appointments, location, address, type, from/to.

17. Military service, branch, from/to status or separation type.

18. Under what specialties or subspecialties do you desire to be listed in the published provider list?

19. What is the complete name of your practice/group?

20. Have you ever been convicted, whether as a result of a guilty plea, a plea of nolo contendere, or verdict of guilty, of a felony, any offense involving moral turpitude, or any offense related to the practice of, or the ability to practice medicine or the related healing arts?

21. Do you have any physical or mental condition, including alcohol or drug dependency which may affect your ability to fulfill your professional responsibilities?

22. Have you ever had such a condition in the past that is now resolved without need for continuing therapy or medication?

23. Have you ever been hospitalized or received any other type of institutional care for such a condition during the last (10) ten years?

24. Are you currently taking medication or under other therapy for a condition which could affect your ability

to fulfill your professional responsibilities if the medication or therapy were discontinued today?

25. Have you ever had privileges with any managed-care organization reduced or terminated for any reason?

The above questions 20–25 should be asked with a place for a "yes" or "no" response. Furthermore, if there is a "yes" response, details should be requested (required).

Licensing/Certifications/Registration numbers:

26. List the name of all states in which you are licensed, registered, certified, or otherwise authorized to practice your specialty.

27. List board certifications (if applicable) by specialty, and include certification date(s) and recertification date(s).

Hospital Privileges:

28. List the name/city/state of all hospital(s) at which you currently hold active, courtesy, or provisional staff privileges, and list the privilege level and each department in which you have clinical privileges. Attach additional pages if necessary.

29. List the name/city/state of all hospital(s) at which you previously held active, courtesy, or provisional staff privileges in the last (10) ten years.

Professional Liability Coverage (at the time this application is completed):

30. Name of your professional liability insurance carrier, policy number, policy period.

31. Have you ever been accused of malpractice or has a suit for any alleged malpractice ever been brought against you? If yes, please provide complete details for each occurrence including allegations, dates, amounts of suits, and amount of any final settlements or judgments on an attached sheet.

32. Has your professional liability insurance ever been canceled, premiums surcharged, or its renewal refused?

Disciplinary Actions:
33. Have you ever been subject to disciplinary review or action, or is pending action, by any of the following:

State Medical/ Professional Licensing Board
Yes _____ No _____ State _____

County or State Medical/Professional Society
Yes _____ No _____ State _____

Hospital or Medical Staff
Yes _____ No _____ Hospital _____

Drug Enforcement Agency
Yes _____ No _____ State _____

Military   Yes _____ No _____ Site _____

Health Care Financing Administration
Yes _____ No _____ State _____

If yes answers are given, make sure to obtain details and followup on them.

Professional References:
34. Please list three professional references with addresses from within the discipline in which you are licensed, registered, certified, or otherwise authorized to practice. If you have practiced in your current community for less than three years, please make sure that one of the references is from your previous community. Also please note that by signing the release enclosed with this application, you are providing (MCO name) with your authorization to verify professional references which may have been provided to others (i.e., hospitals) when being credentialed there. If we cannot obtain these references, it may cause your application to be delayed, pended, or even denied.

35. We would appreciate you attaching a current black and white photograph to be used in any future physician brochures.

Office Information:

> Here, you may want applicants to provide the following office and practice information, which will be helpful in the orientation of their office staff.

36. Name of office manager or contact person.

37. Billing address.

38. Days/hours in office.

39. What are your provisions for after hours care?

40. Do you have 7 days-a-week, 24-hour backup or call coverage?

41. Indicate who you use for backup coverage.

42. Indicate the age range of patients you will treat.

43. If you are a family practitioner or general practitioner, do you handle _____pediatrics? _____obstetrics? _____gynecology? _____geriatrics?

44. Do you use nonphysician practitioners in your office practice?   Yes _____   No _____

45. If yes, are they covered by your professional liability insurance?   Yes _____   No _____

46. What other licensed personnel work in your office?

47. Please indicate to whom you refer most of your patients for the following:

Surgery

Obstetrics

Cardiology

Urology

Ophthalmology

Orthopedics

Gastroenterology

ENT

Oncology

Psychiatry

Family/general practice

Lab and pathology

Radiology

Finally, add some language for the releases and signatures such as: "I hereby certify the above information is true and accurate, and I understand that any material mis-statements in or omissions from this application shall constitute good cause for denial of eligibility, or result in a later termination as a contracted or employed provider of care for (MCO name)."

Also it may help to use the following as a release of information language for reference checks: "I have applied to (MCO name), for eligibility to contract as a member of the (MCO). I hereby authorize [insert name], and its representatives to consult with the administration and members of the medical staffs of hospitals, institutions, professional licensing/registration/certification bodies, professional liability insurance carriers, and professional organizations with which I have been associated and with others who may have information bearing on my professional competence, character, and ethical qualifications. I hereby further consent to the inspection by [MCO name] and its representatives of all documents and information that may be material to an evaluation of my professional qualifications and competence.

By signing this authorization, I release from liability all representatives of [reference name], as well as all representatives of hospitals, institutions, professional licensing/registration/certification bodies, and professional organizations for their acts performed in good faith and without malice in connection with both the exchange of information as consented to above, as well as in connection with evaluating my application, my credentials, and my qualifications. A photocopy of this authorization is to be accepted with the same authority as this original."

Still another release may be necessary to obtain information about professional liability insurance and a Certificate of Coverage. This one is simple and needs to contain some statement such as: "I hereby authorize [insurance company] at [address] to issue a copy of my current Certificate of Coverage to [MCO name], including any notification of any changes in my policy and notification of any future actions which may be filed against me."

It is also a good idea to create a document check list for each credentialing file. One that I use for my new MCO startup clients looks like the following list:

_____ Two copies of the Provider Services Agreement (both completed and signed)

_____ Credentialing Application

_____ Information Sheets

_____ Medical License

_____ DEA Certificate

_____ Malpractice insurance declaration pages showing amounts of coverage

_____ Board Certification Certificates

_____ Peer recommendation (letters)

_____ Residency Certificates, if not board certified

_____ Internship Certificates, if not board certified

_____ Medical School Graduation Certificate

_____ Photograph

With this much information and the true primary source verification, you should be well on your way to developing a good credentialing policy and procedure for any organization, whether an IPA, PHO, or MSO.

CHAPTER

Utilization Management/ Program Development

These two committees should be developing a knowledge of how payors think from the very start. First remember three concepts:

- Utilization equals expense instead of revenue.
- Patient satisfaction is the key to renewed premiums.
- The appropriate care at the appropriate level at the appropriate place at the appropriate time by the appropriate provider is paramount to success.

An insured's benefit equals expense and risk exposure to the payor's bottom line. Therefore, for your organization to represent benefit and attractiveness to a payor, you must be able to manage utilization and also show your management plan on paper.

FIRST THINGS FIRST

To start an organization and make sense of your provider service agreements, you will have to have at least the framework of a utilization management policy on paper. Following is an outline of the elements that must go into these documents:

Utilization Management Program Outline

    I. Statement of Purpose

    II. Objectives

        A. Monitor medical needs of each patient

        B. Monitor the level of care

        C. Ensure appropriate resource management

        D. Develop and evaluate normative data

        E. Analyze global payor trends

        F. Study statistical data and use information to guide the organization

        G. Monitor effect of policy change

        H. Recommend further policy development as required

    III. Participants

        A. Board of directors

        B. Medical director

        C. Members

        D. Support staff

        E. UM committee

        F. Tenure of each position

    IV. Confidentiality Policy

    V. Conflict of Interest Policy

    VI. Plan Reappraisal

    VII. Activities to be studied and frequency of each study

These policies should be in accordance with Milliman and Robertson's *Healthcare Management Guidelines* since that is what most of the health plans in the nation rely upon for a basis of decision-making. Milliman and Robertson is an actuarial firm based in Seattle with offices in most major cities. I have found the team in Denver to be most helpful to my clients, but you may look them up in the Yellow Pages under "Actuarial Consultants" in your town, and if there are not any, call the Denver office for assistance.

The quality assurance and quality improvement must equally be prepared. Its own outline for a program should be developed along the lines of the following outline:

Quality Improvement and Assurance Program

I. Statement of Purpose
   A. Monitor and evaluate quality of care
   B. Pursue opportunities for improvement
II. Plan Activities
   A. Pre-contract onsite review
      1. Review tool to be used
      2. Summary and action plan relative to findings
   B. Patient complaint procedure
      1. Objective
      2. Procedure
      3. Findings and related action plans
   C. High risk reviews
      1. Objective
      2. Procedure
      3. Summary and action plan relative to findings
   D. Adverse outcome review
      1. Objective
      2. Procedure
      3. Summary and action plan relative to findings
   E. Medical records management and documentation quality
      1. Participating provider documentation review
      2. Procedure
      3. Evaluation tool
      4. Summary and action plan relative to findings
III. Participants
   A. Board of directors
   B. Medical director
   C. Members
   D. Support staff
   E. UM committee
   F. Tenure of each position
IV. Confidentiality Policy
V. Conflict of Interest Policy
VI. Plan Reappraisal

Activities to be Studied and Frequency of Each Study

Keep in mind that you will most likely be asked the following questions by the health plans that deal with you:

Frequently Asked Questions by the Health Plans

- Has the National Committee of Quality Assurance, American Association of Preferred Providers, or other external organization reviewed your organization? Has a self-assessment been conducted?
- Please provide a copy of the results of the most recent assessment.
- Please give a brief description of your current quality improvement initiatives including the method used, data sources, and any changes in the outcome that have resulted.
- Please describe in detail your credentialing process for providers and facilities.
- What quality-of-care services measures are used?
- Do you routinely obtain peer evaluation as part of the credentialing and recredentialing process? If so, describe the process.
- For credentialing purposes, how do you evaluate pending malpractice cases and physicians undergoing substance abuse treatment? What followup procedures are in place?
- Is there a functioning Utilization Management/Quality Assurance Committee? How often do they meet?
- Please attach a list of the names and specialties of the physicians who are on the Network's Utilization Management/Quality Assurance Committee(s).
- What are the responsibilities of the Utilization Management/Quality Assurance Committee?
- If the Utilization Management Committee is a separate committee please address each individually.
- What criteria are used by the Utilization Review and Quality Assurance Committees to assess the quality of the care provided by the organizations with which the network has contracted?

- What reports does your administration system produce to allow the Utilization Review and Quality Assurance Committees to evaluate performance?
- Indicate the specific role of outcome measures in the delivery of care within your group. Provide samples of the instruments used to collect patient-reported outcomes information.
- Indicate the specific clinical areas in which outcomes have been (or are currently being) assessed and provide results (whatever available) for each area.
- Describe the benefits which have been derived from the systematic assessment of outcomes.
- If condition or procedure-specific outcome studies have not been completed, please provide the rationale and outline any pertinent future plans.
- Describe any constraints concerning the systematic study of patient outcomes, which health plan should be mindful of an outline, suggested approaches to addressing these constraints.
- Identify the clinical areas in which your group would be prepared to implement outcome studies at the outset of the proposed program.
- Indicate the physician-specific quality indicators currently tracked within your group.
- Describe the method(s) by which the data is adjusted for severity of illness or otherwise risk-stratified.
- Provide the summary quality indicator reports for the last two calendar years.
- Describe the specific process (and provide example) which promotes the continuous improvement in healthcare delivery as evidenced by improvement in quality indicators over time.
- Indicate the approach used to systematically analyze and compare clinical practice, procedure results, and quality indicators.
- If the data is not tracked, please provide the rationale and outline any pertinent future plans.

- Describe the circumstances (protecting individual identity) surrounding any physician who had their privileges limited or revoked, or any group staff member who was disciplined or dismissed as a result of the QM program.
- Describe three examples which demonstrate the effectiveness of the QM program, outlining the underlying issue, the method used to identify and quantify it, the specific intervention, and the reassessment process.
- Describe the methods currently used to assess patient satisfaction with the services provided by your group and provide a sample of the instrument.
- Provide a summary of the results of the last *two* patient satisfaction surveys.

Medical Records Quality Management

In addition, the medical records documentation guidelines for your network organization should probably mirror the NCQA standards as well. The evaluation tool most often includes the following questions:

- Do all pages contain patient ID?
- Is there biographical/personal data?
- Is the provider identified on each entry?
- Are all entries dated?
- Is the record legible?
- Is there a completed problem list?
- Are allergies and adverse reactions to medications prominently displayed?
- Is there an appropriate past medical history in the record?
- Is there a pertinent history and physical exam?
- Are lab and other studies ordered as appropriate?
- Are working diagnoses consistent with findings?
- Are plans of action/treatment consistent with diagnoses?
- Is there a date for a return visit or other followup plan for each encounter?

- Are problems from previous visits addressed?
- Is there evidence of appropriate use of consultants?
- Is there evidence of continuity and coordination of care between primary and specialty care physicians?
- Do consultant summaries, lab, and imaging study results reflect primary care physician review?
- Does the care appear to be medically appropriate?
- Is there a completed immunization record?
- Are preventive services appropriately used?

Adverse Outcome Review

Another task you may endeavor as a committee is to select certain criteria to monitor for outcomes that in some instances, may have never needed to progress to such a high level of acuity, had the appropriate intervention been initiated at the appropriate time, namely:

- Cancer of the breast (female)
- Cancer of the cervix
- Cellulitis
- Cancer of the colon or rectum
- Diabetic coma/ketoacidosis
- Gangrene (angiosclerotic)
- Hemorrhage secondary to anticoagulation
- Hypertensive crisis
- Hypokalemia due to a diuretic
- Mal-union/non-union of a fracture
- Perforated or hemorrhaging ulcer
- Pregnancy induced hypertension
- Admitting diagnosis of pulmonary embolism
- Readmission within 14 days for same diagnosis
- Ruptured appendix
- Admitting diagnosis of septicemia
- Status asthmaticus
- Dehydration of a child under age two

• Low birth weight/prematurity less than 2500 grams
• Urinary tract infection

Finally, in both committee programs be sure to add in some language about due process and arbitration or mediation in the event that someone who was the subject of the review disagrees with the outcome and findings and perhaps the decisions made. NCQA requires that there be a grievance mechanism for all accredited health plans, therefore, your network should mirror this policy as well. You will be well on your way to establishing the network as one who is serious about managing quality and utilization while rendering appropriate patient care. Now that you have seen the outlines, go to work. And remember, I expect you to make a protocol that is better for me as a patient than what my insurance company would design. After all, you folks are the trained healthcare practitioners, you know quality or lack thereof when you see it!

NETWORK MANAGEMENT

Finance, Utilization Management/Capitated Risk Management

As an IPA, PHO, or MSO usually takes capitated risk, this chapter has been designed more as a reference and planning tool for any of the three groups and is modeled for physicians and administrators. Nonphysician providers may find many of the reports useful as well to stimulate reports that mirror these but that are more germane to their area of specialization. These reports will also give you a great start on outcomes reporting for internal management and marketing.

Lets start with the basics. Often I find that medical practices, especially primary-care practices that are already assuming capitated risk do not close out their month end reports as they should. Therefore, forgive the elementary level of this early part of the chapter, but I have learned to assume nothing. I also have been made painfully aware that in the PHO setting, if the billing and financial management team is "borrowed" from the hospital side, often, the physician and other nonhospital billing issues are foreign to most hospital billing experts, and therefore, they find it difficult to truly manage capitation.

For these reports, I have blended my experience as a practice manager, hospital business office coordinator, and my HMO reporting capability background from my stint in provider relations of a large HMO capitated plan. These are the reports I have found most helpful. Most every one can be achieved by using *Microsoft Access* or another relational database software tied to a centralized data depository at an MSO or similar venue.

Finance

Monthly and Annual Aged Trial Balances   A network-wide report demonstrating the accounts receivable status in the following format:

> Patient's last name, first name, middle initial, responsible party
> Current balance at: 0-30 days, 31-60, 61-90, 91-120, 120-150, 151-180
> Employer Name, Payor ID, Subscriber ID, Group ID, home phone, work phone

Monthly, Quarterly, and Annual Adjustments to Open Balances   This is usually a report detailing all accounts receivable adjustments made as debit adjustments.

Monthly-Quarterly Insurance Receiveables Grouped by Payor   Current-30 days, 31-60, 61-90, 91-120, 121-150, 151-180, 181-120 for all fee for service reimbursements expected. Listed by patient and date of service.

Monthly and Quarterly Collections Status Report   A report showing what has been done to collect receivables due, pended claims, suspended claims, notations on the account, who has worked on the account, and the present status and/or recommendations.

Monthly, Quarterly, and Annual Paid -To- Billed Ratios (discounted fee for service claims)   A report showing the present day status of all reimbursement for all payors using discounted fee-for-service methods.

Monthly Collections Activities by Billing Specialist

Monthly and Quarterly Suspended Claims Reports

Monthly, Quarterly, and Annual Paid-To-Billed Ratios—Capitation   This is a report showing the ratio of revenue collected through capitation, copayments, fee for service for noncovered services of an elective or cosmetic nature, against what would have been collected using a standard conversion rate for productivity-based reimbursement on an encounter-by-encounter only basis.

For all of the payor categories—Medicare, Medicaid, commercial, and others, including Tricare, Workers' compensation, and motor vehicle accident/Personal Injury (MVA/PI) related plans. The report is then presented by individual capitated provider in the following format:

Provider Name, MM/YY, Health Plan Name, Paid-to-Billed Ratio   The chart below may be of help for those of you unfamiliar with this method of monitoring profitability.

In order to derive your paid-to-billed ratios you have to calculate the following information:

ABC Health Plan

Step One:

$34,000	capitation revenue paid
$ 240	copayments and deductibles paid
$ 1,305	elective and non-covered services paid by patients (paid, not charged and in A/R!)
$35,545	total health plan derivative revenue

Step Two:

$35,545	total health plan derivative revenue
$26,405	actual billed services at usual and customary charges

Step Three:

134.6%	paid to billed ratio

(Note that good capitated performance is in the 130%-160% paid-to-billed range)

Utilization Management Reports

Monthly and Quarterly Procedure Rate Frequency for All Primary Care Providers by Practice and by Individual Physician   Analysis by physician of all evaluation and management codes used in encounters and billings regardless of reimbursement type.

Monthly and Quarterly Procedure Rate Frequencies by Special Procedures by PCP and by Specialty (IM, FP, Peds)   Analysis of procedural frequencies for certain in-office procedures, that is, otic lavage, EKG, spirometry, pap smears, biopsies, etc.

Quarterly Procedure Rate Frequencies by Referral Specialists/Others Analysis of evaluation and management codes used for each physician, grouped by specialty.

Quarterly Procedure Rate Frequencies by Referral/Specialists for Procedures Ordinarily Done by PCPs   Analysis of procedural frequencies for certain in-office procedures, that is, otic lavage, EKG, spirometry, pap smears, biopsies, etc.

Month-To-Date and Year-To-Date Utilization by Provider A report showing each physician's productivity on a monthly basis by CPT code reported.

Quarterly Formulary Compliance by PCP   A report showing formulary compliance rates by network and referral physicians, including out-of-network physicians. This report should show only individual performance. Layout should be by drug category that is, antihistamines, antibiotics, analgesics, etc. Reports should also contain peer comparisons.

Further detail would be helpful showing any patients who are in stoploss or catastrophic categories listing patient name, date of birth, identification number, medications utilized and diagnoses reported from claims experience as a trailer report. This report would be helpful for the physicians and case management team to be able to closely examine and re-evaluate patients on complex polypharmacy with concomitant disorders.

Quarterly Formulary Compliance by Referral Physician This report should include all specialists in all classifications who may prescribe drugs to patients for covered conditions for which an active referral is on file from a network physician. Layout should be by physician, by drug category, and should include utilization data inclusive of any drugs prescribed which were noncompliant with the established formulary, and drugs which are classified as potentially habit-forming or highly controlled.

UM/ QI Reports

Monthly and quarterly laboratory/pathology specimens with normal results in greater than 10% of specimens;

Monthly and quarterly pathology specimens requiring repeat examination(s), listed by submitting physician;

Quarterly and annual preventive medicine deficiencies;
   Mammography, by patient and age
   Well woman examinations not performed
   Immunizations overdue—childhood and adult boosters
   Prenatal visits missed

Monthly anaphylaxis ED presentations by physician;

Monthly unscheduled return to OR by physician, with reason stated;

Monthly post-operative complications by physician, with reason stated;

Quarterly Listings of Patients identified with the following diagnoses:

Alzheimer's	Hypertension
Asthma	Inflammatory Bowel Disease
Atrial Fibrillation	Irritable Bowel Disease
CHF	Lupus
Chronic Low Back Pain	Migraine
CVA	Myocardial Infarction
Depression	Neoplasm
Diabetes	Obesity
Fibromyalgia	Osteoporosis
GERD	Pregnancy
Hypercholesterolemia	Renal Failure

Rheumatoid Arthritis	TIA
Stroke	Tonsillitis

This report will enable the medical director and medical management/case management team to more closely coordinate appropriate resources for the patients and to reduce uncoordinated care for these patients as they often have concomitant disorders.

Monthly—Hospital admissions by DRG, by patient, by age, by admitting physician;

Monthly—Length of stay by DRG, by patient, by age, by admitting physician;

Monthly—Percent diagnosis seen by gender, by age, by zip code;

Quarterly—Admits for surgery by physician, by LOS, by day of the week, by principal procedure:
    Knees, hips, CABG, shoulders

Quarterly—Specialist peer comparisons, by billed charges, by specialty, by diagnosis.

The report is helpful in determining who sees the patient more frequently with the same outcome for the same diagnosis with a higher or lower cost basis per diagnosis as related to visit frequency.

Visits PTMPY for the following diagnoses by PCPs (collectively):

Alzheimer's	Irritable
Asthma	Migraine
Bowel Disease	Myocardial Infarction
CHF	Neoplasm
Chronic Low Back Pain	Obesity
CVA	Osteoporosis
Depression	Pregnancy
Diabetes	Renal Failure
GERD	Stroke
Hypercholesterolemia	TIA
Hypertension	Tonsillitis
Inflammatory Bowel	
Disease	

Visits PTMPY for the following diagnoses by specialists (collectively):

Alzheimer's	Irritable Bowel Disease
Asthma	Lupus
Atrial Fibrillation	Migraine
CHF	Myocardial Infarction
Chronic Low Back Pain	Neoplasm
CVA	Obesity
Depression	Osteoporosis
Diabetes	Pregnancy
Fibromyalgia	Renal Failure
GERD	Rheumatoid Arthritis
Hypercholesterolemia	Stroke
Hypertension	TIA
Inflammatory Bowel Disease	Tonsillitis

In conclusion, it is necessary to have the claims data flowing through a centralized repository to monitor all of these items on a routine basis. It is also helpful to have a full-time nurse manager in the department that will run these reports and note any aberrances. This nurse should have a certified case manager (CCM) background, loads of experience, and the actual CCM credential. Once the reports are prepared and reviewed by the nurse manager, he/she can prepare synopsis reports for the appropriate committees to review at the committee level and at the board level. It would be wise to copy your marketing committee with these periodic reports as well for their review and strategic planning purposes.

8

CHAPTER

Medicare Changes That Will Affect Network Development

The Health Care Financing Administration (HCFA) has begun a demonstration project aimed at expanding the types of managed-care plans available to Medicare beneficiaries and testing different payment methods, such as partial capitation. The Medicare Choices demonstration is one of several elements of the President's plan designed to expand managed-care options for Medicare beneficiaries and improve Medicare payment methods for managed-care plans, including a competitive bidding demonstration.

HCFA began soliciting contractor support for three other elements of this initiative. These include design of Medicare competitive bidding demonstration; development of a marketing strategy to inform beneficiaries of Medicare choices; and studies of managed-care issues, such as development of access measures that are appropriate for managed care. HCFA invited a wide range of managed-care plans to participate in its Choices demonstration, including preferred provider organizations (PPOs), health maaintenance organizations (HMOs), and integrated delivery systems (IDSs). Currently, most Medicare managed-care contracts are with HMOs. Applications were especially sought from such managed-care plans in Hartford CT; Philadelphia, PA;

Atlanta, GA; Jacksonville, FL; New Orleans, LA; Columbus, OH; Louisville, KY; Houston, TX; and Sacramento, CA where HCFA believed that these markets had the greatest potential for expanding choices to Medicare beneficiaries based on available options in the private sector. The administration's commitment to expanding voluntary choices for Medicare beneficiaries believe it was important to experiment with a wide variety of types of plans. While they were targeting these markets, they also agreed to accept other types of innovative applications from other areas. For example, they wanted applications from plans offering to extend their networks to rural communities and plans emphasizing primary care case management procedures. To participate in the demonstration, all plans must:

- Have networks that can provide the full range of Medicare Part A and Part B services;
- Demonstrate financial viability and be willing to bear some risk, however, HCFA will consider a variety of payment arrangements;
- Have a well-developed quality assurance program; and
- Have demonstrable data systems capability, including the ability to produce encounter data or the ability to work with HCFA to produce such data.

As of January 1, 1997, more than 4.9 million Medicare beneficiaries were enrolled in a total of 336 managed-care plans, accounting for 13% of the total Medicare population. That represents a 108% increase in managed-care enrollment since 1993. In 1996, an average of 80,000 Medicare beneficiaries voluntarily enrolled in risk-bearing HMOs each month. Keep in mind that Medicare beneficiaries can enroll or disenroll in a managed-care plan at any time and for any reason with only 30 day notice.

Managed-care plans can serve Medicare beneficiaries through three types of contracts: risk, cost, and healthcare prepayment plans (HCPPs). All plans receive a monthly payment from the Medicare program.

Risk plans are paid a per capita premium set at approximately 95% of the projected average expenses for fee-for-services beneficiaries. Risk plans assume full financial risk for all care provided to Medicare beneficiaries. Risk plans must provide all Medicare-covered services, and most plans offer additional services, such as prescription drugs and eyeglasses. With the exception of emergency and out-of-area urgent care, members of risk plans must receive all of their care through the plan. However, as of January 1, 1996, risk plans can provide an out-of-network option that, subject to certain conditions, allows beneficiaries to go to providers who are not part of the plan. Since January 1, 1993, enrollment in risk plans has grown more than 170%. Currently, 86% of Medicare beneficiaries in managed care are in risk plans. As of January 1, 1997, risk plans made up 248 of the 350 managed-care plans participating in Medicare.

Cost plans are paid a pre-determined monthly amount per beneficiary based on a total estimated budget. Adjustments to that payment are made at the end of the year for any variations from the budget. Cost plans must provide all Medicare-covered services but do not provide the additional services that some risk plans offer. Beneficiaries can also obtain Medicare-covered services outside the plan without limitation. When a beneficiary goes outside the plan, Medicare pays its traditional share of those costs and the beneficiary pays Medicare's coinsurance and deductibles.

Health Care Prepayment Plans (HCPPs) are paid in a similar manner as cost plans but only cover part of the Medicare benefit package. HCPPs do not cover Medicare Part A services (inpatient hospital care, skilled nursing, hospice, and some home healthcare) but some do arrange for services and may file Part A claims for their members.

Nationally, three-fourths of beneficiaries have a choice of at least one managed-care plan while more than half have a choice of two or more plans. Medicare managed-care enrollment varies greatly depending on geographic location. The majority of beneficiaries enrolled in such plans live in California, Florida, Oregon, New York, Arizona, and Hawaii.

HCFA launched the "Medicare Choices" demonstration project designed to allow beneficiaries to join a wider variety of managed-care plans and to extend managed-care options to rural areas. Enrollment is now underway in six participating plans. They include four provider sponsored networks (PSNs), a preferred provider organization (PPO), and a "triple option" hybrid that lets members see gatekeeper physicians, other plan providers without going through the gatekeeper, or providers outside the plan. An additional 13 demonstration plans are expected to begin enrollment during 1997. This "Choices" project is also testing new payment methods, such as partial capitation and adjustments based on the actual health needs of beneficiaries.

The differentiating factor that I see in the present design of PSNs is that they can contract with the federal government to enroll Medicare beneficiaries. However, as Bruce Fried explained at the TIPAA annual conference in New Orleans in March 1997, presently the network holding the contract must control at least 70% of the expenditures. Therefore, the Management Service Organization (MSO) or the hospital is in the position to drive the PSN, by contract, rather than a physician organization. Other than that, it seems that very evolved PHOs will be sitting in the "catbird seat" to receive appointments in rural areas that are selected by HCFA for participation in the Medicare Choices Demonstration Project.

THE PHYSICIAN INCENTIVE PLAN

A final rule on physician incentive plans (PIP) in Medicare and Medicaid Managed Care Organizations (MCOs) was published in the Federal Register on March 27, 1996. A corrected final rule was published in the Federal Register on September 3, 1996 that delayed implementation beyond the date originally called for in the final rule. However, implementation dates appearing in the September 3, 1996 corrected notice did not change.

Legislative action to regulate PIPs was enacted in the Omnibus Budget Reconciliation Acts (OBRA) of 1986 and 1987. However, these laws were superseded by Sections 4204(a) and 4731 of the OBRA of 1990. Statutory authority for this rule can be found in Sections 1876(I)(8), 1903(m)(2)(A)(x), and 1903(m)(5)(A)(v) of the Social Security Act (the Act).

For MCOs with an existing contract with HCFA or agreement with a state, the first five of seven disclosures listed below must be made by the contract renewal date. January 1, 1997 is the date for MCOs with Medicare risk contracts. For Medicaid

MCOs and Medicare cost contracting MCOs, this will be the contract renewal or anniversary date that falls on or after January 1, 1997. MCOs must also be compliant with stop-loss requirements on these same dates. Conducting a beneficiary survey (if required) must be done within one year of the five item disclosure. Disclosure of data related to capitation payments had to be made by April 1, 1997 for all contracts in effect during calendar year 1996. Contracts made effective on or after January 1, 1997 must submit capitation data beginning April 1 of the year following the initial effective date of the contract. More information related to time frames for compliance is included throughout this document.

A PIP is defined by HCFA as "any compensation arrangement between an MCO and a physician or physician group that may directly or indirectly have the effect of reducing or limiting services furnished to Medicare beneficiaries or Medicaid recipients enrolled in the MCO." The compensation arrangements negotiated between subcontractors of an MCO (for example, physician-hospital organizations, IPAs) and a physician or group are of particular importance, given that the compensation arrangements with which a physician is most familiar will have the greatest potential to affect the physician's referral behavior. For this reason, all contracting tiers of the MCO's arrangements are subject to the regulation.

The physician incentive rule applies only to those PIPs that base compensation (in whole or in part) on the use or cost of referral services. PIPs that base compensation entirely on the direct furnishing of services by a physician or group, or on factors unrelated to the use or cost of services to beneficiaries (for example, on member satisfaction or physician participation in quality assurance activities) are not subject to this rule. The physician incentive rule applies only to Medicare risk and cost-based contracts, Medicaid HMOs, and those health insuring organizations contracting under Medicaid that are subject to §1903(m) of the Social Security Act. Other organizations, such as Health Care Prepayment Plans under Medicare or Prepaid Health Plans under Medicaid are not subject to this regulation, however, these beneficiaries may be included in the pooling when determining substantial financial risk or stop-loss insurance.

Prohibition of Certain Physician Payments

PIPs may not include any direct or indirect payments to physicians or groups as an inducement to limit or reduce necessary services furnished to an individual enrollee who is covered under the MCO's contract. Indirect payments include offerings of monetary value (such as, stock options or waivers of debt) measured in the present or future. It should be understood that this prohibition does not preclude an MCO from encouraging its contracted physicians to authorize only those services that are medically necessary.

Disclosure Requirements

Information Disclosed

The disclosure requirements apply not only to an MCO's direct contracting arrangements with providers, but to its subcontracting arrangements as well. Physician groups that do not transfer substantial financial risk (SFR) to their own employees or members need only disclose this fact. But for physician groups that do transfer SFR, and for all other contracting relationships regardless of the level of risk transferred, the following pieces of information are required by the regulation:

1) Whether referral services are covered by the PIP. If only services furnished by the physician or group are addressed by the PIP, then there is no need for disclosure of other aspects of the PIP;

2) Type of arrangement (for example, withhold, bonus, capitation);

3) Percent of total income at risk for referrals;

4) Amount and type of stop-loss protection;

5) Panel size and whether enrollees were pooled in order to achieve the panel size;

6) In the case of capitated physicians or groups, percentage data from the previous calendar year showing how capitation payments paid to primary care physicians were used to pay for primary care services, referral services to specialists, hospital services, and

other types of providers (for example, nursing home, home health agencies); and

7) If the MCO is required by this regulation to conduct a customer satisfaction survey, a summary of the survey results.

Note that this regulation differentiates between physician groups and "intermediate entities" that contract between MCOs and physician groups. Intermediate entities must disclose upon their incentive arrangements, regardless of the level of risk that may be transferred in those arrangements. Examples of intermediate entities include individual practice associations (IPAs) that contract with one or more physician groups, as well as physician-hospital organizations. IPAs that contract only with individual physicians and not with physician groups are considered physician groups under this rule.

When Disclosure to Regulators Must Be Made

Initial disclosure of the first five items listed previously must be made by the contract renewal or anniversary date in 1997, or prior to a new contract's initial effective date. Subsequent reporting of these five elements is required annually thereafter. Reporting of the sixth item related to capitation payments began on April 1, 1997, for all contracts that were in effect in calendar year 1996. Contracts made effective on or after January 1, 1997 must report capitation data by April 1 of the year following the contract's initial effective date. The seventh item, summary survey results, should be submitted to regulators within a reasonable period of time after conduct of the survey—generally four months.

Disclosure to Beneficiaries

For Medicare or Medicaid beneficiaries who request it, contracting MCOs must provide information indicating whether the MCO or any of its contractors or subcontractors uses a PIP that may affect the use of referral services, the type of incentive arrangement(s) used, and whether stop-loss protection is provided. If the MCO is required to conduct a survey, it must also provide beneficiary requestors with a summary of survey results.

Substantial Financial Risk (SFR) Defined:

According to the final rule, if a PIP puts a physician or physician group at "substantial financial risk" for referral services: *(1)* the MCO must survey current and previously enrolled members to assess member access to and satisfaction with the quality of services, and *(2)* there must be adequate and appropriate stop-loss protections.

The amount at risk for referral services is the difference between the maximum potential referral payments and the minimum potential referral payments. Bonuses unrelated to referrals (for example, quality or access bonuses such as those related to member satisfaction or physician open panels) should not be counted towards referral payments. Potential payments is defined as the maximum anticipated total payments that the physician/group could receive if use or costs of referral services were low enough. Payments may be for either direct or referral services, or for administration, but do not include bonuses paid for reasons other than referrals. The most recent year's utilization, cost experience, and any current or anticipated factors affecting payment amounts may be accounted for in determining potential payments, but may not be accounted for in determining the amount at risk for referral services. In order to determine the amount at risk for referrals, the theoretical amount at risk should be used. If there is no specific dollar or percentage amount noted in the incentive arrangement, then the PIP should be considered as potentially putting 100% of the potential payments at risk for referral services.

The SFR threshold is set at 25% of "potential payments" for covered services, regardless of the frequency of assessment (that is, collection) or distribution of payments. SFR is present when the 25% threshold is exceeded. The following incentive arrangements should be considered as SFR:

1) Withholds greater than 25% of potential payments;
2) Withholds less than 25% of potential payments if the physician/group/ intermediate entity is potentially at risk for amounts exceeding 25% of potential payments;

3) Bonuses that are greater than 33% of potential payments minus the bonus. This is the equivalent of 25% of potential payments if you were to include the bonus itself;

4) Withholds plus bonuses if the withholds plus bonuses equal more than 25% of potential payments. The threshold bonus percentage for a particular withhold percentage may be calculated using the formula— Withhold % = − 0.75 (bonus %) + 25%;

5) Capitation arrangements if the difference between the maximum and minimum possible payments is more than 25% of the maximum possible payments, or if such arrangements are not clearly explained in the physician/group's contract; or

6) Any other arrangement that could hold a physician/group/intermediate entity liable for more than 25% of potential payments.

Large Patient Panels and Substantial Financial Risk

If a physician group's patient panel is greater than 25,000 patients, then the PIP is not considered to put the group or its participating physician(s) at SFR because the risk is spread over the large patient panel. The 25,000 patients may be a pool of Medicare, Medicaid, and commercial members across the MCOs that have contracted with the physician group. However, the physician group can only pool categories of patients for which the following criteria are true:

Referral risk must have been transferred in each of the physician incentive arrangements applicable to the pooled enrollees;

The incentive arrangements related to the compensation for those enrollees must be comparable with respect to the nature and extent of the risk borne;

The payments for all pooled enrollees must be held in a common risk pool;

The distribution of payments from the risk pool must not be calculated separately by patient category or by MCO, and

No provider contracts can require that risk be segmented by MCO or by patient category.

The pooling of patients calculation will be relevant to one of two scenarios. The calculation may show that the physician group serves more than 25,000 patients and, therefore, is able to spread referral risk over a wide enough patient base so that stop-loss protection is not needed. Or the calculation will show that the physician group serves 25,000 or fewer patients, in which case stop-loss is required if the incentive arrangements put the group at substantial financial risk. If per patient (as opposed to aggregate) protection is obtained, the group's pooled patient panel size would determine how much stop-loss to acquire.

Requirements when SFR is determined that follows:

1. *Surveys*—When a MCO's physicians or groups are put at substantial financial risk, the MCO must survey its current Medicare/Medicaid enrollees as well as those who disenrolled in the last 12 months (for reasons other than loss of eligibility or relocation outside of the MCO's service area). If a survey is required, it must be conducted within one year of the date on which the MCO is required to disclose the five elements noted previously. It must be conducted annually thereafter for as long as physicians or groups are placed at SFR. The survey may be of a sample population, but must be designed, implemented, and analyzed in accordance with commonly accepted principles of survey design and statistical analysis. Survey questions must address enrollee/disenrollee satisfaction with access to services (including referral services) and quality of care.

2. *Stop Loss Protection*—Stop-loss protection must be in place to protect physicians and/or physician groups to whom substantial financial risk has been transferred. (Entities at higher contracting levels are not required to have stop-loss, even if SFR is transferred in the contracts affecting those entities.) The MCO may either provide stop-loss directly, purchase it, or let the physician/group purchase it. Either aggregate or per patient stop-loss may be acquired. The rule specifies that if aggregate stop-loss is provided, it must cover 90% of the cost of referral services that exceed 25% of potential payments. Physicians and groups can be held liable for only 10%. If per patient stop-loss is acquired, it must be determined based on the physician or physician group's patient panel size and cover 90% of the referral costs which exceed the following per patient limits:

Patient panel size	1–1000	1001–5000	5001–8000	8001–10,000	10,001–25,000
Single combined limit	$6000*	$30,000	$40,000	$75,000	$150,000
Separate institutional limit	$10,000*	$40,000	$60,000	$100,000	$200,000
Separate professional limit	$3000*	$10,000	$15,000	$20,000	$25,000

*The asterisks in this table indicate that, in these situations, stop-loss insurance would be impractical. Not only would the premiums be prohibitively expensive, but the protections for patients would likely not be adequate for panels of fewer than 500 patients. MCOs and physician groups clearly should not be putting physicians at financial risk for panel sizes this small. It is our understanding that doing so is not common. For completeness, however, we do show that the limits would be in these circumstances.

The institutional and professional stop-loss limits above represent the actuarial equivalents of the single combined limits. The physician group or MCO may choose to purchase whatever type is best suited to cover the referral risk in the incentive arrangement.

Enforcement

For Medicare HMOs and CMPs that are not in compliance with the requirements of this rule, HCFA may apply intermediate sanctions or the Office of Inspector General may apply civil money penalties, as described in 42 CFR Section 417.500 (revised). Intermediate sanctions and civil money penalties, as described in the revised Section 434.67 of 42 CFR, may also be applied to Medicaid Health Insuring Organizations (HIOs) and risk comprehensive HMOs found out of compliance with the rule. Federal financial participation (FFP) is only available for Medicaid payments to contractors and subcontractors that comply with this rule. HCFA may also withhold FFP if either a state or contractor/subcontractor fails to fulfill state plan or contract requirements, respectively. Withholding of FFP is also allowed if a state fails to collect from an HIO or HMO proof of that contractor's compliance with the rule.

Frequently Asked Questions About the Physician Incentive Plan Ruling

The following questions and answers were supplied by the Health Care Financing Administration. I thought that they mirrored quite well the questions I had been asked about the legislation. The answers come verbatim from HCFA and I am pleased to be able to include them in this discussion.

PHYSICIAN INCENTIVE PLAN REGULATION QUESTIONS AND ANSWERS
Substantial Financial Risk Definition

In specific terms, substantial financial risk is set at greater than 25% of potential payments for covered services, regardless of the frequency of assessment (that is, collection) or distribution of payments. The term "potential payments" means simply the maximum anticipated total payments that the physician or physician group could receive if the use or cost of referral services were significantly low.

The cost of referrals, then, must not exceed that 25% level, or else the financial arrangement is considered to put the physician or group at substantial financial risk. For example, say a doctor contracts with an MCO and that MCO holds back a certain amount of the doctor's pay (for example, $6 per member per month). The MCO will give the doctor the $6 per member per month only if the cost of referral services falls below a targeted level. Those $6 are considered to be "at risk" for referral services. The amount equals the difference between the maximum potential referral payments and the minimum potential referral payments (but does not include bonus payments unrelated to referral services). It is put into the numerator of the risk equation. The denominator of the risk equation equals the maximum potential payments that the doctor could receive for direct or referral services, or administration. Therefore, if the same doctor receives $24 per member per month for the primary care services he provides, and is subject to the $6 withhold, the risk equation is as follows:

Risk level: $6/24 = 25\%$ not substantial financial risk

In addition to the stop-loss insurance, the MCO must provide a survey of patient satisfaction that includes information from current enrollees and disenrollees.

Note: If a physician group's patient panel is more than 25,000 patients, then that physician group is not considered to be at substantial financial risk, its arrangements do not trigger the need for a beneficiary survey, and the group is not required by the regulation to have stop-loss protection. For the purpose of making this determination, the patients of the group can be pooled across MCOs and across Medicare, Medicaid, and commercial enrollees if specific criteria are met. See Question 5 in this document's section on stop-loss protection.

QUESTIONS AND ANSWERS

Substantial Financial Risk

Question 1: For purposes of calculating substantial financial risk, are ancillary services considered referral services?

Answer: If the physician group performs the ancillary services, then the services are not referral services. If the physician group refers patients to other providers (including independent contractors to the group) to perform the ancillary services, then the services are referral services. In contrast, services provided within the physician group are not considered referral services.

Question 2: Why is the threshold for substantial financial risk set at 25%? This level seems too high.

Answer: The following factors are among those that determined the 25% threshold: Information available to HCFA at the time the regulation was developed indicated that the average withhold used by plans was between 10% and 20%. As indicated in the proposed rule, we determined that an outlier approach was preferred and that we wanted to consider anything that exceeded the average as substantial risk; actuarial data supported this value; and physicians typically give up to 25% discounts to preferred customers.

Question 3: Did HCFA consider using a 20% risk threshold?

Answer: Yes. We considered a range of percentage thresholds. We also received comments in favor of both higher and lower thresholds. The information available to us indicates that the 25% threshold provides adequate protection to beneficiaries. We estimate that between one-third and one-half of all physician compensation arrangements will exceed this threshold. We will continue to monitor this issue.

Question 4: How does the regulation affect provider groups that are licensed in a state and are allowed to accept full risk?

Answer: The regulation does not prohibit groups from accepting full risk for all health services. It requires appropriate parties to ensure that adequate stop-loss is in place and to conduct beneficiary surveys.

Question 5: *(a)* If a physician is paid straight capitation (that is, uses no withholds or bonuses) and that capitation covers services that the physician does not provide, would the physician be at substantial financial risk? *(b)* What if the MCO has a performance history of three or five years and can show that its physicians have not lost more than 25% of the capitated amount?

Answer: Yes, this situation would be one of substantial financial risk, because the risk is not limited. If a capitation has no limit on the referral risk, it essentially equals 100% risk (with potentially greater risk).

Regarding the use of past history as a means of predicting future behavior, such experience is no guarantee of future referral behavior or the future healthcare needs and costs of the current enrollees served.

Question 6: Does the determination of risk apply only to Medicare and Medicaid covered benefits, or if the MCO provides additional benefits at its own expense, should these be included in the determination?

Answer: All payments related to referral services furnished to enrolled Medicare or Medicaid beneficiaries are to be included in the risk determination, even if those services are not Medicare or Medicaid covered services. This regulation's requirements apply to contracts serving persons covered under a Medicare risk or cost contract, Medicaid HMO contract, or certain Medicaid Health Insuring Organizations (HIOs). These regulations do not apply to incentive arrangements applicable to Medicare enrollees who are covered by the MCO through an employer group (for example, working aged and their dependents), those who are not enrolled in a Medicare risk or cost contract, and those Medicaid beneficiaries enrolled in Prepaid Health Plans or HIOs that are not subject to Section 1903(m) of the Social Security Act.

Question 7: Will HCFA include quality bonuses in the denominator of the equation for substantial financial risk?

Answer: No. The regulation currently does not include quality bonuses as a factor in the substantial financial risk calculation. Although HCFA supports the concept of quality bonus payments, limited information exists on their effectiveness as an incentive to provide quality healthcare. HCFA acknowledges that some MCOs believe that the current regulation may create a disincentive for them to adopt quality-based bonuses. However, we are willing to revisit this issue in the future after more information is available on the use of such bonuses and the extent to which they are used effectively. To assist HCFA in considering this matter, MCOs and their subcontractors are asked to voluntarily submit information about the use of quality bonuses in addition to the required disclosure information.

Hypothetical Situations

Question 8: Would a physician be at substantial financial risk if his/her MCO's annual payment to him/her for services and administration total $100,000 and the organization withholds 25% (or $25,000) to cover deficits in the referral or inpatient hospital pool? Assume the MCO does not hold the physician liable for referral costs that exceed the withhold.

Answer: No. The physician is not at substantial financial risk because he/she was not at risk for more than 25% of payments.

Question 9: Please clarify how substantial financial risk is determined when various risk arrangements are used. For example, say an MCO pays its doctors $100 per member per month and puts $24 at risk through a withhold, then the same doctors are part of a physician-hospital risk pool where they can get $50 if utilization goals are met. Is the risk seen as 24/100, 50/50, 74/150, or something else?

Answer: The risk is 74/150 and therefore the doctors are at substantial financial risk. That number is arrived at by adding the amount at risk for referral services (here, the amounts of the withhold and hospital pool or (24 + 50) then dividing by the amount of maximum potential payments (150).

Question 10: If a contractor capitates a physician group comprised of physicians (for example, psychiatrists) and nonphysicians (for example, other mental health providers), would the calculation to determine substantial financial risk assumed by the group change if the group is comprised exclusively of physicians?

Answer: No. As long as physicians are part of the group and the contracted services include physician services, the calculation of the amount of risk transferred to the physicians remains the same.

Question 11: Would a physician be at substantial financial risk in the following example? An MCO's annual payments to this physician total $100,000 and the MCO imposes a 20% withhold ($20,000) for referrals. In addition, the MCO holds the physician liable for up to $5000 of any referral costs not covered by the withhold. The physician's referrals total $35,000, exceeding the withhold by $15,000; however, the MCO does not hold its physicians liable for amounts over 25% of payments (or $25,000).

Answer: No, the physician is not at substantial financial risk because the risk is limited to $25,000. However, if the MCO held the physician liable for all amounts over the withhold (instead of limiting liability to $5000 for referral costs not included in the 20% withhold), then the physician would have been at substantial financial *risk. This is because, having accrued referral costs of $35,000, he/she would have exceeded the 25% risk threshold by $10,000.*

Question 12: Is a physician at substantial financial risk if his/her payments from the MCO total $75,000, he/she does not exceed utilization targets for referral and inpatient hospital services, but he/she is eligible for a $25,000 bonus (33% of $75,000).

Answer: No, because this physician's bonus did not exceed the limit of 33% of potential payments, not counting the bonus itself (in other words, 25% of the potential payments if you included the bonus as part of the potential payments). However, any incentive arrangement other than a bonus alone must be no greater than 25% of potential payments or else it will be considered as substantial financial risk.

Question 13: What if an MCO has the following arrangement: A physician is not permitted to keep any savings from the referral account. Then if referrals cost less than $100,000, the physician must return the remainder of the referral account to the MCO. If referral costs are more than $100,000, he/she may be liable for up to 25% of the capitation for his/her own services. The contract clearly states the following: If referrals exceed $125,000, the physician will receive no less than $75,000. If referrals are less than $100,000, the physician will receive no more than $100,000. Is this physician at substantial financial risk?

Answer: No. The difference between the highest possible payments ($100,000) and the lowest possible payments ($75,000) is no more than 25% of the maximum payments (here, the difference is $25,000), therefore the physician is not at substantial financial risk.

Stop-Loss Protection

Definition: Organizations whose contracts or subcontracts place physicians or physician groups at substantial financial risk must ensure that those providers have either aggregate or per-patient stop-loss protection. The aggregate stop-loss protection requires coverage of at least 90% of the costs of referral services that exceed 25% of potential payments. The per-patient stop-loss protection requires coverage of 90% of the costs of referral services that exceed specified per-patient limits.

Question 1: What does stop-loss protection mean?

Answer: Stop-loss is a type of insurance coverage designed to limit the amount of financial loss experienced by a healthcare provider. An MCO or physician group normally buys this insurance so that, if the liabilities of the MCO or group exceed what is expected based on prior experience, the insurer will "stop" further losses by paying the liabilities which exceed either a total dollar (aggregate) amount, or a per patient amount.

Question 2: Is the MCO required to provide stop-loss protection to physicians or physicians groups at substantial financial risk?

Answer: The final rule held the MCO accountable for stop-loss insurance by requiring it to either provide the stop-loss itself or reimburse physician groups for the cost of stop-loss purchased by them to cover costs attributable to the MCO's enrollees. HCFA originally planned to require MCOs to provide proof that they paid for the insurance. Based on industry comments and our understanding of industry practices, we have concluded that we do not need to mandate how the payment for stop-loss insurance is arranged. The MCO merely needs to provide assurance to either HCFA or the State Medicaid Agency that the proper stop-loss protection is in place.

Question 3: Does stop-loss protection apply only to referral services?

Answer: Generally, stop-loss protection applies to the costs of all services furnished by a physician or physician group. For the purposes of this regulation, however, stop-loss coverage must cover at least 90% of the costs of referral services above the substantial financial risk threshold. The physician or physician group is liable for no more than 10% of the remaining referral costs above the threshold.

Question 4: If a MCO or physician group chooses to obtain per-patient stop-loss protection for the purposes of this regulation, what are the appropriate per-patient stop-loss deductibles, or attachment points, that are required?

Answer: Changes were made to the per-patient deductible amounts listed in the March 27, 1996, final rule with comment. Recognizing that greater variation exists in the type of stop-loss policies used than was allowed by the March rule, HCFA has revised the rule to allow the provision of either a single combined limit or separate limits for professional and institutional services. We have also revised the categorization of patient panel size to increase the number of categories and smooth out the gradation of attachment points. Based on actuarial analyses and consultation with experts knowledgeable about current stop-loss insurance practices, we have revised these limits as indicated in the following table:

Patient panel size	1–1000	1001–5000	5001–8000	8001–10,000	10,001–25,000
Single combined limit	$6000*	$30,000	$40,000	$75,000	$150,000
Separate institutional limit	$10,000*	$40,000	$60,000	$100,000	$200,000
Separate professional limit	$3000*	$10,000	$15,000	$20,000	$25,000

*The asterisks in this table indicate that, in these situations, stop-loss insurance would be impractical. Not only would the premiums be prohibitively expensive, but the protections for patients would likely not be adequate for panels of fewer than 500 patients. MCOs and physician groups clearly should not be putting physicians at financial risk for panel sizes this small. It is our understanding that doing so is not common. For completeness, however, we do show that the limits would be in these circumstances.

Question 5: Why do stop-loss limits increase as panel size increases? Are the plans providing more protection as panel size increases?

Answer: As patient panel size increases, stop-loss protection under the per-patient stop-loss requirement decreases. That is because with increasing panel size, payments to a physician or physician group increase and the element of risk decreases with the increased payments thus a physician group with a panel size of 15,000 patients has more income with which to sustain a financial loss and, therefore, requires less stop-loss insurance than would a group with income generated only due to 5000 patients.

Question 6: Does aggregate stop-loss take panel size into account?

Answer: Yes. To the extent that aggregate stop-loss limits require coverage of 90% of the costs of referral services that exceed 25% of potential payments, those limits reflect payments based on panel size.

Question 7: Under what circumstances is pooling permissible for purposes of determining the appropriate stop-loss limit?

Answer: The Medicare, Medicaid, and commercial enrollees of one or more MCOs served by a physician group may be pooled as long as certain criteria are met. The pooling of patients calculation will be relevant to one of two scenarios. The calculation may show that the physician group serves more than 25,000 patients and, therefore, is able to spread referral risk over a wide enough patient base so that stop-loss protection is not needed. Or the calculation will show that the physician group serves 25,000 or fewer patients, in which case stop-loss is required if the incentive arrangements put the group at substantial financial risk. If per patient (as opposed to aggregate) protection is obtained, it must be for the single combined or separate professional and institutional limits shown above. In this case, the group's pooled patient panel size would determine how much stop-loss to acquire.

Pooling of patients across MCOs and/or patient categories (for example, Medicaid, Medicare, commercial) is allowed only if the following five criteria are met:

- *Referral risk must have been transferred in each of the physician incentive arrangements applicable to the pooled enrollees;*
- *The incentive arrangements related to the compensation for those enrollees must be comparable with respect to the nature and extent of the risk borne;*
- *The payments for all pooled enrollees must be held in a common risk pool;*

- *The distribution of payments from the risk pool must not be calculated separately by patient category or by MCO; and*
- *No provider contracts can require that risk be segmented by MCO or by patient category.*

Question 8: If the capitation rate or fee-for-service schedule is different between three lines of business due to the expected differences in healthcare needs and resultant costs for the Medicare, Medicaid, and commercial populations, does this mean these patients cannot be pooled?

Answer: No, but specific criteria must be met in order to pool patients across product lines and/or across MCOs. See Question 7 above.

Disclosure

Question 1: If an MCO agrees to provide stop-loss and to conduct surveys, must they still disclose the information to HCFA as required by the regulation?

Answer: Yes, pursuant to the regulation, MCOs must still disclose the information. This information serves many purposes. It will be used to monitor compliance, evaluate the impact of the regulation, and to ensure the delivery of high quality healthcare. In enacting this legislation, Congress clearly intended MCOs to disclose at least some information about the nature of physician incentive compensation arrangements and the extent to which physicians are being placed at substantial risk by the arrangements.

Question 2: It seems that the information disclosed pursuant to the regulation is proprietary and should be protected under the Freedom of Information Act (FOIA). What information is proprietary?

Answer: For information submitted to HCFA, a precise determination of what is proprietary information cannot be made until we have reviewed specific FOIA requests. At that time, the FOIA office will request that the plan involved specify what it feels is proprietary and the office will then determine what is proprietary. An MCO may, if it so desires, designate the information as proprietary at the time of submission. Requests will be evaluated on a case-by-case basis, balancing the needs of the party to protect proprietary information against the public interest in disclosing information that will serve the goals of the regulation. After several cases have been reviewed, we will publish general guidance in manual publications describing what is proprietary information. For MCOs disclosing to State Medicaid Agencies, individual states' rules regarding the protection of proprietary information will apply. HCFA will also publish aggregate information that summarizes the more sensitive details of incentive plans. At a minimum, basic information will be available to the public. Such information will include items such as whether or not an incentive plan covers referral services, what type of incentive arrangements (for example, withhold or capitation) are used by a MCO or its subcontractors, whether adequate stop-loss protection is in place, and the summary results of any surveys required by the regulation.

Question 3:   Will disclosure to beneficiaries of financial incentives information be required at the time of their enrollment? Also, will MCOs be allowed broad discretion to decide how the information is presented?

Answer: MCOs will be required to publish in the evidence of coverage (EOC) notices, or such other notice as approved by the applicable HCFA Regional Office or the State Medicaid Agency, that beneficiaries can request summary information on the MCO's physician incentive plans. These EOC notices are available at enrollment, therefore, the information will be available to patients upon enrollment. The nature of the disclosure to beneficiaries will be general, as opposed to providing physician-specific financial incentives information. Materials must convey information about the types of incentives used in contracts affecting physicians in the MCO's network. MCOs will not be required to disclose for each beneficiary requesting it the details of the particular incentive arrangement under which that beneficiary's physician operates. MCOs will be allowed some discretion in crafting language to convey the required information to beneficiaries. A separate document of recommended language for beneficiary materials is available from HCFA or your State Medicaid Agency.

Question 4: Will subcontractors to the MCO be allowed to attest that they have no physician incentive plan or no physician incentive plan related to the use of referral services for Medicare or Medicaid enrollees? If so, will MCOs be able to rely upon these attestations without need for a further audit of the subcontractor's compensation arrangements (assuming the MCO has no reason to believe the attestation may be false)?

Answer: Yes. Reporting entities will be allowed to make such attestations and MCOs will not be required to conduct validation audits unless they have reason to believe the attestation or other information submitted by a subcontractor is false.

Question 5: Will HCFA facilitate the survey requirement by using such items as a standard survey questionnaire, detailed instructions on survey design and/or a comparative report card?

Answer: The final rule did not specify that the plans must conduct a specific survey for this regulation because most plans already administer surveys that meet the requirements of this regulation. In late spring of 1997, the Office of Managed Care (OMC) will conduct a nationwide consumer satisfaction survey of Medicare beneficiaries in MCOs. All Medicare contracting plans that meet the criteria set for inclusion (for example, have had a Medicare contract for at least one year) are expected to be required to participate. The primary purpose of the survey is to provide information to consumers that enable them to plan comparisons and ultimately make more informed choices.

This survey will be administered by a third-party contractor to HCFA. This contractor will use the Consumer Assessments of Health Plans Study (or CAHPS survey), under development by the Agency for Health Care Policy and Research (AHCPR). The contractor will survey a random sample of Medicare beneficiaries in each participating MCO. The CAHPS survey, which has modules for use with Medicare, Medicaid, and commercial enrolled populations, addresses the basic requirements of the regulation: it includes questions regarding access, quality, and satisfaction.

By participating in the CAHPS survey, a Medicare MCO will be able to meet the survey requirement related to enrollees without having to conduct its own survey. MCOs and states should note, however, that neither the current Medicare nor Medicaid CAHPS surveys contain modules for disenrolled members. The CAHPS disenrollee modules will be available for both Medicaid and Medicare in 1998. In the meantime, in order to facilitate MCOs' compliance with the requirement for a survey of disenrollees, HCFA will supply standardized disenrollment surveys and sampling specifications for MCOs to self-administer in 1997. A separate document providing guidance in development of a survey is available from HCFA or your State Medicaid Agency.

With regard to the Medicaid program, the CAHPS survey includes a Medicaid version that can be separately administered to Medicaid enrollees. This instrument will yield data that meet the requirements of the regulation. Although HCFA will not require that the CAHPS survey be administered for Medicaid MCOs, states will have the option to make such a requirement.

Question 6: Will the surveys that are required as part of the disclosure requirement include questions about referral problems?

Answer: Yes. The surveys should include questions that deal with referral problems.

Question 7: What are the specifications on release of the beneficiary surveys?

Answer: The surveys are required of all MCOs whose contracts or subcontracts place physicians or physician groups at substantial financial risk. They are required to be conducted within one year of an MCO's initial disclosure to HCFA or a State Medicaid Agency. They will be required annually thereafter. Summary survey results must be submitted to regulators and to any beneficiary who requests the information of an MCO.

Question 8: For purposes of the disclosure requirement, who does the term "beneficiaries" include?

Answer: The term refers to persons receiving Medicare and/or Medicaid benefits. It includes potential enrollees, current enrollees, and disenrollees of MCOs contracting with the Medicare or Medicaid programs.

Question 9:   Regarding disclosure to enrollees, how does this regulation fit in with HCFA's policy of fully informing beneficiaries?

Answer: In the preamble, we encouraged MCOs to disclose to beneficiaries. We considered the possibility of requiring the disclosure rather than only making the information available upon request by beneficiaries. We are not sure, however, that the level of interest in this information on the part of beneficiaries, and its value to them, warrants such a requirement. In the coming year, we will be providing all Medicare beneficiaries with comparable information about the services and quality of care provided by their managed-care organizations. In addition, we support and encourage interaction between consumer advocacy groups and MCOs as a means of disseminating information to beneficiaries.

Question 10:   Does the disclosure requirement apply to all MCOs or just those putting doctors at substantial financial risk?

Answer: It applies to all MCOs. However, if an MCO has a subcontract with a physician group and the group's contract with its physician members does not place those members at substantial financial risk, then the MCO does not need to disclose any details on the incentive arrangements between the group and its members. Financial arrangements between physicians or groups and any other entities (for example, PHOs, the MCO) must be disclosed, regardless of whether or not the physician or group is at substantial financial risk.

Question 11:   *(a)* What about Pools of Doctors (PODs) (that is, groups of independent physicians who are aggregated into a single risk pool by an MCO or PHO), that are not actually private corporations like a physician group or an IPA? Would they need to report if the POD includes PCPs only sharing risk for their own services? *(b)* What about if the POD includes PCPs and specialists sharing risk for their services as a POD? *(c)* Finally, would PODs need to report if comprised of PCPs, specialists, hospital, and ancillary services?

Answer: In all three instances, some reporting would need to occur, but the extent of the disclosure would vary. In the first two examples, the MCO would simply report that the POD was not at risk for services it did not provide. In the third example, disclosure would need to detail the types of risk arrangements used (for example, capitation, withhold, bonus), the percent of total potential income at risk for referrals, and if that percentage exceeded 25%, information about stop-loss protection.

Miscellaneous

Question 1: Why was Congress concerned about physician incentive plans?

Answer: As we indicated in the March 27, 1996 final rule (page 13434), Congress was concerned with ensuring that under-use of necessary services does not occur. We believe the final rule implements the federal law to ensure adequate protection of Medicare and Medicaid beneficiaries so that they have access to all necessary and appropriate care.

Question 2: What was the purpose of a comment period with the March 27, 1996 final rule?

Answer: This rule applies to Medicare HMOs and competitive medical plans and Medicaid HMOs and those Health Insuring Organizations subject to Section 1903(m) of the Social Security Act. However, the provisions of this rule may also affect entities that would not have been affected at the time we published the proposed rules (December 14, 1992). This is because of the physician self-referral rules in Section 1877 of the Social Security Act, as amended by the Omnibus Budget Reconciliation Act of 1993. Section 1877 provides that a physician (or an immediate family member of the physician) who has a financial relationship with certain entities may not make a referral for designated health services to that entity for Medicare or Medicaid beneficiaries. Various exceptions to this referral prohibition exist. Under certain circumstances, a physician can use compliance with the physician incentive regulations in order to be excepted from the referral ban. Thus, entities not directly affected by the physician incentive rule may now be affected by it due to the physician self-referral ban. The additional entities potentially affected include preferred provider organizations, MCOs that do not contract with Medicare or Medicaid and are not federally qualified, Prepaid Health Plans that contract under Medicaid, and some Medicaid managed-care programs authorized under Sections 1915(b) or 1115 of the Social Security Act. As a result, we issued the March 27, 1996 rule as a final rule, but permitted a period for public comment to accommodate new entities potentially affected by the rule. Based on the public comments we received, we will be issuing a revised final rule in the near future.

Question 3: Do the physician incentive plan final rules apply to both Medicaid Federally Qualified HMOs and State-Plan Defined HMOs?

Answer: The rules apply to Medicaid prepaid organizations subject to Section 1903(m) of the Social Security Act, including both Federally Qualified HMOs and State-Plan Defined HMOs, as well as certain Health Insuring Organizations (HIOs). Those HIOs not subject to 1903(m) (namely, HIOs that began operating prior to January 1, 1986, and California county-sponsored HIOs eligible for exemption from 1903(m) due to Section 4734 of the Omnibus Budget Reconciliation Act of 1990) are not subject to the physician incentive rules.

Question 4: Where in the law or regulations is information available on the physician self-referral ban?

Answer: Section 13562 of the Omnibus Budget Reconciliation Act of 1993 (OBRA '93) amended Section 1877 of the Social Security Act to incorporate the physician incentive plan rules as part of the physician self-referral ban. Under the provisions, compliance with the physician incentive plan rules will be necessary to meet the

*exemption for personal services arrangements if a personal ser-
vices compensation arrangement involves compensation that
varies based on the volume or value of referrals. To qualify for this
exemption, an organization or person must also meet several other
conditions. See Section 1877(e)(3). We are developing regulations
to implement the physician self-referral ban provisions.*

Question 5: Do the physician incentive plan rules apply to
Medicaid prepaid health plans (PHPs), particularly behavioral
health PHPs?

*Answer: While the physician incentive plan rules, for purposes of
Medicaid prepaid contracts, apply only to Medicaid organizations
subject to Section 1903(m) of the Social Security Act (and PHPs
are not subject to Section 1903(m)), the physician self-referral ban
requirements incorporate physician incentive plan rules as indicated above. The physician self-referral ban, as it applies to the
referral for "designated health services" applies to PHPs, including behavioral health PHPs, if physician compensation varies
based on the volume or value of referrals. Therefore, physicians
in a PHP will need to comply with the physician incentive plan
rules if they wish to receive the personal services exception from
the physician self-referral ban regulation once that regulation goes
into effect.*

Question 6: How do the physician self-referral ban rules apply to
states' Medicaid managed-care programs under Section 1115
waivers?

*Answer: HCFA has granted several states the authority for their
Medicaid managed-care contracts to not be subject to some of the
provisions in Section 1903(m) of the Social Security Act. HCFA
could choose to use this waiver authority to exempt Medicaid MCO
or HIO contracts in a state from the physician incentive plan rules.
However, given the quality concerns at the heart of this regulation,
it is unlikely that HCFA would choose to waive this particular requirement for states operating 1115 programs.*

Question 7: What is HCFA doing in the area of quality measures?

Answer: HCFA is working with the National Committee on Quality Assurance to refine the Health Plan Employer Data and Information Set (HEDIS) 2.5. We are also working with the American Public Welfare Association (APWA) to implement the HEDIS 3.0 measures which were released in June 1996. We expect these measures to be implemented in June 1997. Finally, HCFA is collaborating with other agencies (Department of Defense, AHCPR) and private sector purchasers to develop and use other quality measures (for example, the Foundation for Accountability).

Question 8: When will HCFA begin monitoring MCO compliance with the physician incentive plan rules?

Answer: The effective date of the physician incentive plan rules was January 1, 1997. The specific compliance date for each MCO depends on when the contract first becomes effective, renews, or has its anniversary date during the 1997 calendar year. We will expect MCOs to make good faith efforts at coming into compliance by their own particular compliance dates.

Question 9: How is a withhold different from capitation?

Answer: Capitation means a set dollar payment per patient per unit of time (usually per month) that an MCO pays a physician or physician group to cover a specified set of services and administrative costs without regard to the actual number of services provided. The services covered may include the physician's own services, referral services, or all medical services. A withhold is the percentage of payments or set dollar amounts that an MCO holds back from a physician or physician group's capitation or fee-for-service payments. This amount may or may not be returned to the physician/group depending on specific predetermined factors.

Question 10: Do the regulations prohibit situations in which the utilization management procedure provides incentives for the use of outpatient services, as appropriate?

Answer: No. As long as the incentives are for the furnishing of outpatient care, as appropriate, there is no such prohibition on these arrangements.

I hope that this section has saved you some time and research. In the event you have more questions regarding this subject area, please contact the Health Care Financing Administration, Department of Health and Human Services, Office of Managed Care.

9

Antitrust Concerns for Provider Networks*

INTRODUCTION

The IPA, PHO, and MSO groups that have been forming in the past few years continue to request information about the federal guidelines for antitrust enforcement policy in healthcare. I find it uncanny that hundreds who have attended both my contracting seminars and IDS Development seminars, state that they are actively engaged in IDS participation or development and have never heard of these documents before. This frightens me for their sake as there is so much increased prosecutorial activity going on these days. You cannot take antitrust rules for granted. This chapter provides a general summary (with many verbatim excerpts) of these guidelines, which were provided in the form of policy statements issued jointly, and subsequently amended, by the United States Department of Justice and the Federal Trade Commission (FTC) between September 1993 and September 1996.

As a paralegal, I cannot provide specific legal advice as to whether your business activity is in compliance with federal

---

*For specific questions about the contents in this chapter please contact your local healthcare attorney.

antitrust law and these guidelines. Moreover, this chapter and the policy statements mentioned do not include any analysis of enforcement policy resulting from legal challenges. This antitrust case law is equally important and relevant when considering any type of business activity. Therefore, I urge you to contact your local healthcare attorney to provide you with further guidance, whenever you are contemplating a business venture that may fall under the purview of the Department of Justice and Federal Trade Commission's jurisdiction.

WHAT ARE THE ANTITRUST LAWS?

First enacted in the 1890s, the purpose of the antitrust laws was to protect consumers against anti-competitive business activities. These activities, especially the creation of monopolies, enabled businesses to charge higher prices to consumers (price fixing). The law simply stated that "every contract combination in the form of trust or otherwise, or conspiracy, in restraint of trade or commerce" was illegal, and every person who shall "monopolize, or attempt to monopolize, or combine or conspire with any other person" was in violation of the law.

Although this law was specifically intended to be a consumer protection measure, ironically, at times, consumers and the marketplace are best served through combined business arrangements and the sharing of information, which may otherwise be interpreted as a monopoly or restriction on trade. This is the paradox of the antitrust laws. Sometimes, one very large business providing goods or services for everyone "gouges" consumers, and the federal government needs to step in (such as, the break-up of AT&T or Standard Oil). Other times, companies merging together can produce business efficiencies and savings to consumers (such as, the recent proposed mergers of some of the "Baby Bell" telephone companies).

The growth and dissolution of companies, as dictated by the antitrust laws, is cyclical, and the interpretation and application of the antitrust laws is constantly evolving. In its application, the government always takes into consideration the nature of the current marketplace, the effect of this marketplace on consumers, and the pricing of goods or services.

Consequently, because some current combined business activities in the healthcare industry have resulted in efficiencies in healthcare delivery and cost-savings to the patient, the United States Department of Justice and the Federal Trade Commission (DOJ/FTC) have provided some guidance as to what activities would not run afoul of the antitrust laws in this new healthcare delivery environment.

Terms Used in the Guidelines

The DOJ/FTC have developed their own terms to describe conduct in the health care industry, and they use these terms to describe what conduct will be considered legal as opposed to illegal. Key terms are as follows:

Physician network joint ventures are physician - controlled ventures in which the network's physician participants collectively agree on prices or price-related terms and jointly market their services. They will be referred to as "physician networks." They include independent practice associations (IPAs), preferred provider organizations (PPOs), and other arrangements. At least some, if not all, of the physicians are assumed to be in independent practices as opposed to group practices where the physicians have merged their practices. These networks are not fully integrated, they are either partially integrated or unintegrated. Therefore, price agreements among physicians in the network amounts to per se illegal price fixing unless the network is sufficiently integrated to qualify for rule of reason analysis.

Multi-provider networks are ventures among providers that jointly market their healthcare services to health plans and other purchasers. They include networks among competing providers as well as networks of providers offering complementary or unrelated services. A physician hospital organization is a multi-provider network. At least some, if not all, of the providers in the network are independent as opposed to being part of the same business entity. Normally these networks are not fully integrated, they are partially integrated or unintegrated.

Antitrust safety zones are categories of physician networks that will not be scrutinized by the DOJ/FTC. The safety zones are defined in the guidelines. However, being within a safety zone does not bar private parties from bringing suit. Safety zones are not laws, and it is possible that a court may disagree with the DOJ/FTC. There are no safety zones for multi-provider networks. Absent extraordinary circumstances, the agencies will not challenge activity that is identified as falling within an antitrust "safety zone," *so long as all specific requirements of that "safety zone" are met.*

For all of these identified antitrust "safety zones," providers can take advantage of the DOJ's expedited business review procedure, or the FTC's advisory opinion procedure as outlined in the Code of Federal Regulations. The agencies will respond to a business review or advisory opinion request within 90 days after all necessary information is submitted by the providers who are considering joining business activities that may fall within a particular "safety zone." The agencies will provide an opinion as to whether the business activity under consideration falls within an antitrust "safety zone." For the addresses and telephone numbers of these agencies, please refer to the last page of this fact sheet.

Per se **violation of antitrust laws** are antitrust laws that consider naked agreements among competitors that fix prices or allocate markets as illegal on their face (that is, a per se violation of the antitrust laws).

Exclusive network is an exclusive physician network that does not allow its member physicians to belong to a competing healthcare delivery network, or which does not allow its members to contract with payors except on terms that the network accepts, or both. Exclusivity may be found to exist because it is expressly required, or it might be found to exist as an implicit agreement, meaning that the physicians do not deal with payors outside of the network or join other networks even though it is not an express requirement. An exclusive network is potentially threatening to competition because its physicians are not available to form competing networks or to participate in managed-care plans through arrangements made outside of the network, therefore, it is treated more restrictively under the antitrust laws.

Nonexclusive network is a physician network that allows its members to contract with competing healthcare delivery networks or to contract individually with payors on terms not accepted by the network. It is not as threatening to competition as an exclusive network, therefore it is treated less restrictively. However, the DOJ/FTC is concerned that a nonexclusive network might actually be an exclusive network in disguise to take advantage of the less restrictive antitrust treatment. To determine whether a network is truly nonexclusive, the DOJ/FTC will look at a number of criteria, including: *(a)* whether viable competing networks or health plans with adequate provider participation exist in the market, *(b)* whether members of the nonexclusive network actually contract with other networks or health plans or whether there is evidence that they are willing to do so, *(c)* whether providers in the nonexclusive network earn substantial revenue outside of the network, *(d)* whether there is evidence that members of the nonexclusive network are "departicipating" from other networks, and *(e)* whether the members of the nonexclusive network coordinate their prices or terms of dealing with other networks or health plans.

Horizontal arrangements are arrangements between competing providers, such as physicians in the same specialty. The antitrust laws are highly restrictive of horizontal arrangements, as it is believed that they are likely to be anti-competitive.

Vertical arrangements are arrangements between providers that perform different services and do not compete, such as hospitals and physicians. The antitrust laws are less restrictive of vertical arrangements because they are usually meant to achieve efficiencies. It should be noted, however, that a vertical arrangement can also have horizontal dimensions. For example, when a hospital makes an arrangement with a physician network, the combined multi-provider network has both vertical relationships between the physicians and the hospital, and horizontal relationships among the physicians. Physicians in a multi-provider network may not engage in price fixing simply because the multi-provider network has a vertical dimension. In addition, a hospital that employs physicians is in competition with independent physicians in the same specialty, and therefore arrangements between the hospital and those competing physicians are horizontal, not vertical.

"Rule of Reason" **analysis** is where competitors for economic efficiency reasons, integrate in a joint venture, such agreements, if

reasonably necessary to accomplish the pro-competitive benefits of the integration, are analyzed under the "rule of reason." What this means is that the agencies will review and evaluate the facts in the particular arrangement under scrutiny, instead of finding it illegal on its face (such as, a per se violation).

Under "rule of reason" analysis, physician networks would not be viewed as being per se illegal so long as two conditions are met:

1) The physicians' integration through the network is likely to produce significant efficiencies that benefit consumers; and

2) Any price agreements (or other agreements that would otherwise be *per se* illegal) by the network physicians are reasonably necessary to realize those efficiencies and fall within the antitrust "safety zone."

As with any other type of antitrust analysis, determining whether an arrangement is merely a vehicle to fix prices or engage in naked anti-competitive conduct, or a device to produce efficiencies and consumer benefits, is a factual inquiry that must be done on a case-by-case basis. Again, the agencies' analysis is to determine the arrangement's true nature and likely competitive effects.

The Federal Guidelines of Antitrust Enforcement Policy in Healthcare

On August 28, 1996, the United States Department of Justice and the Federal Trade Commission (FTC) jointly released antitrust guidelines for the healthcare industry. These guidelines expand upon, and clarify, the guidelines which were first issued in September 1993, and revised and expanded in September 1994.

During the last several years, the healthcare marketplace has been rapidly changing. During this time of tremendous change, there was a great deal of uncertainty concerning the federal government's antitrust enforcement policy. Prior to 1993, some believed that this enforcement policy actually was inhibiting mergers and joint activities that enhanced patient healthcare delivery and controlled the cost to the consumer. Consequently, in September 1993, the Justice Department and the FTC released antitrust guidelines to provide some guidance to healthcare providers and hospitals, so that they could enter into joint ventures, mergers, and other collaborative activities without violating the antitrust laws.

These original guidelines included six policy statements on hospital mergers; hospital joint ventures involving high-technology or other expensive medical equipment; hospital participation in exchanges of price and cost information; physicians' provision of information to purchasers of healthcare services; healthcare providers' joint purchasing arrangements; and physician network joint ventures.

At that time, the Department of Justice and FTC made a commitment to issue expedited business review or advisory opinions in response to requests for antitrust guidance on specific proposed healthcare arrangements.

The 1994 guidelines, which superseded the 1993 statements, added new policy statements, including: hospital joint ventures involving specialized clinical or other expensive healthcare services; providers' collective provisions of fee-related information to purchasers of healthcare services; and analytical principles relating to a broad range of healthcare provider networks ("multiprovider networks"). It also expanded the antitrust "safety zones" for several of the 1993 policy statements.

Since 1994, the Department of Justice and the FTC have gained much experience with arrangements involving joint provider activity, and therefore, have once again provided further clarification. The August 1996 guidelines, which are almost 150 pages in length, expanded the enforcement policy statement on physician network joint ventures and the more general statement on multi-provider networks.

These most recent guidelines from August 1996, which supersede the previous policy statements, are now comprised of nine policy statements of which we will examine those five antitrust enforcement policy guidelines which concern physician and other providers' activities:

Statement 4   Providers' Collective Provision of Non-Fee-Related Information to Purchasers of Healthcare Services

Statement 5   Providers' Collective Provision of Fee-Related
               Information to Purchasers of Healthcare Services
Statement 6   Provider Participation in Exchanges of Price and
               Cost Information
Statement 7   Joint Purchasing Arrangements Among
               Healthcare Providers
Statement 8   Physician Network Joint Ventures
Statement 9   Multi-provider Networks

Let us examine these statements individually:

Statement 4—Providers' Collective Provision of Non-Fee-Related Information to Purchasers of Healthcare Services

The agencies have designated an antitrust "safety zone" where competing providers can collect and share non-fee-related information, when they meet certain requirements. Providers can collectively share underlying medical data that may improve the mode, quality, or efficiency of treatment, and this activity is unlikely to raise any significant antitrust concerns. Statistics such as outcome data, or practice parameters may be collected by providers, and they may collectively engage in discussions with purchasers about the scientific merit of that data.

This "safety zone" specifically excludes any attempt by providers to coerce a purchaser's decision-making by implying or threatening a boycott of any plan that does not follow the providers' joint recommendation.

Statement 5—Providers' Collective Provision of Fee-Related Information to Purchasers of Healthcare Services

The agencies have designated an antitrust "safety zone" for the collective sharing of fee-related information by competing providers, when they meet certain requirements. With reasonable safeguards in place, competing healthcare providers can collectively provide to purchasers factual information concerning the fees charged currently and in the past, as well as other factual information concerning the amounts, levels, or methods of fees or reimbursement.

In order to qualify for this "safety zone," the collection of information to be provided to purchasers must meet **all** of the following requirements:

a) The collection is managed by an unaffiliated third party (such as, a healthcare consultant or trade association);

b) Any information that is shared among or is available to the competing providers furnishing the data must be more than three months old; and

c) For any information that is available, there are at least five providers reporting data upon which each disseminated statistic is based; no individual provider's data may represent more than 25% on a weighted basis of that statistic; and any information disseminated must be sufficiently aggregated so recipients cannot identify the prices charged by any individual provider.

This antitrust "safety zone" does not apply to collective negotiations between nonintegrated providers and purchasers relating to any agreement among the providers on fees or other terms or aspects of reimbursement, or to any agreement among integrated providers to deal with purchasers only on agreed terms. Also, providers cannot collectively threaten or engage in a boycott or similar conduct to coerce any purchasers to accept collectively-determined fees.

Also, specifically excluded from this "safety zone" are providers' collective provisions of information or views concerning prospective fee-related matters.

Statement 6—Provider Participation in Exchanges of Price and Cost Information

The agencies have designated an antitrust "safety zone" for provider participation in the exchange of price and cost information, when they meet certain requirements. Absent extraordinary circumstances, providers can participate in written surveys of prices for healthcare services, or wages, salaries, or benefits of healthcare personnel, so long as:

a) The survey is managed by an unaffiliated third-party (such as a healthcare consultant or trade association);

b) The information provided by the survey participants is based on data more than 3 months old; and

c) There are at least five providers reporting data upon which each disseminated statistic is based; no individual provider's data represents more than 25% on a weighted basis of that statistic, and any information disseminated is sufficiently aggregated so recipients cannot identify the prices charged or compensation paid by any particular provider.

Any other exchanges of price and cost information that fall outside this antitrust "safety zone" will be evaluated to determine whether the information exchange may have an anti-competitive effect that outweighs any pro-competitive justification for the exchange. Such surveys, including public, nonprovider initiated surveys, may not raise competitive concerns. However, exchanges of future prices for provider services, or future compensation of employees, are very likely to be considered anti-competitive. It is illegal to exchange among competing providers price or cost information that results in an agreement among competitors regarding the prices for healthcare services or the wages to be paid to healthcare employees.

Statement 7—Joint Purchasing Arrangements Among Healthcare Providers

The agencies have designated an antitrust "safety zone" for competing providers to enter into joint purchasing arrangements (such as, for the purchase of computers or pharmaceutical products) when they meet certain requirements. These joint purchasing arrangements may allow the participants to achieve efficiencies that benefit consumers by lowering the cost of healthcare.

These joint purchasing arrangements are unlikely to raise antitrust concerns unless the arrangement accounts for such a large portion of the purchases of a product or service that the participants can effectively exercise market power in the purchase of the product or service; or the products or services being purchased jointly account for so large a proportion of the total cost of the services being sold by the participants that the joint purchasing arrangement may facilitate price fixing or otherwise reduce competition.

Absent extraordinary circumstances, the agencies will not challenge joint purchasing arrangements among healthcare providers, so long as two conditions are met:

a) The purchases account for less than 35% of the total sales of the purchased product or service in the relevant market; and

b) The cost of the products and services purchased jointly accounts for less than 20% of the total revenues from all products or services sold by each competing participant in the joint purchasing arrangement.

Joint purchasing arrangements among healthcare providers that fall outside of the antitrust "safety zone" do not necessarily raise antitrust concerns. There are several safeguards that joint purchasing arrangements can adopt to avoid some antitrust "pitfalls" and demonstrate that the joint purchasing arrangement is intended to achieve economic efficiencies, rather than to serve anti-competitive purposes:

a) Members should not be required to use the arrangement for all of their purchases of a particular product or service (however, voluntarily specified amounts are acceptable, so that a volume discount or other favorable contract can be negotiated);

b) Negotiations should be conducted on behalf of the joint purchasing arrangement by an independent employee or agent who is not also an employee of any participant; and

c) Communications between the purchasing group and each individual participant should be kept confidential, and not discussed with, or disseminated to, other participants.

It is not necessary to open a joint purchasing arrangement to all competitors in the market. However, if some competitors excluded from the arrangements are unable to compete effectively without access to the arrangement and competition is subsequently stifled, this activity may raise antitrust concerns.

Statement 8—Physician Network Joint Ventures

The agencies have designated several "antitrust safety zones" for physician network joint ventures, when they meet certain requirements. A physician network joint venture is a physician-controlled venture in which the network's physician participants collectively agree on prices or price-related items and jointly market their services (such as, individual practice associations (IPAs) and preferred provider organizations (PPOs)).

Use of the Messenger Model to Negotiate an Agreement with a Payor

Please note: These scenarios and determinations of legality are verbatim from Frequently Asked Questions provided by the DOJ/FTC. They are presented as informational and do not constitute legal or professional advice. Antitrust laws are always decided on case specifics.

Characteristics of the Arrangement   About 35% of the physicians in a community decide that they want to negotiate an agreement with a payor, but they want to avoid the bar on price fixing. They decide to appoint a third party to act as a "messenger" in negotiations with the payor. The messenger will collect information from each of the physicians about the fee range that the physician is willing to accept, and each physician will give the messenger authority to accept contract offers from payors that fall within or above the fee range desired by the physician. The messenger will share the fee range desired by any physician with the other physicians. The messenger will aggregate the information and create a schedule showing what percentages of physicians will accept contract offers at various fee levels.

The messenger will then present the schedule to payors and solicit offers. Offers that fall within or above the fee range of any physician will be accepted on the physician's behalf. Offers that do not fall within a physician's fee range will be forwarded to the physician, and the physician may accept or reject the offer. The messenger will not tell any physician whether other physicians intend to accept an offer or not, but will provide physicians with objective information about any offer, including how it compares with the offers of other payors and the meaning of contract terms. The physicians will not discuss any contract offers among themselves. Once the messenger obtains the responses of the physicians, that data is relayed to the payor, and contracts are finalized.

Legality of the Arrangement Statement 9 defines this type of arrangement as the "messenger model" and says that it may be used, although it does not define a safety zone for it. These characteristics must be strictly adhered to in order to stay within the law. Statement 9 warns that variations may cause the arrangement to be price fixing.

The section on the messenger model in Statement 9 does not place any size limits on non-integrated groups that use it. The DOJ has issued a pair of consent judgments involving physician hospital organizations (PHOs) which say that the PHOs, both of which include very large percentages of physicians in their markets, may legally use the messenger model to arrive at fee arrangements with payors.[1] In addition, officials of the Department of Justice have publicly stated that they do not see a reason to place limits on the percentage of physicians that can participate in a messenger model arrangement. The rationale for that position is that there is no agreement among the physicians, therefore there is no joint venture subject to limits on its market power. However, if a messenger model arrangement involves more than an arrangement to arrive at fees, and also involves agreements among physicians to conduct their practices pursuant to certain terms, those agreements may make the arrangement a joint venture, at least with respect to the matters on which there is an agreement among the physicians. In that event, limits on the size of the joint venture may apply.

Statement 9 of the 1996 guidelines says that horizontal networks of all kinds will be subjected to review under the "Horizontal Merger Guidelines" to determine whether they have

---

[1] U.S. v. Health Choice of Northwest Missouri Inc., Civil Action No. 95-6171-CVSJ6, U.S.D.C. W. D. Mo., Final Judgment and Competitive Impact Statement, 9/13/95; U.S. v. Healthcare Partners. Inc., Civil Action No.: 395-CV-01946RNC, U.S.D.C., D. Conn., Final Judgment and Competitive Impact Statement, 9/13/95.

too much market power. These guidelines set forth a methodology for calculating market shares for competing businesses, and then set forth a methodology for determining whether a merger between two or more of the competing businesses would result in an illegal aggregation of market power.

Variations on the Messenger Model   This model is cumbersome and expensive to use. Therefore, physicians often wish to push the envelope of the model by adopting shortcuts that reduce the amount of time that must be invested. Some of these variations are as follows:

- **Variation:** Same facts as above, except that the messenger "jawbones" payors that make offers that do not fall within the preauthorized fee ranges of most of the physicians and have to be relayed back to them for acceptance or rejection. The messenger tries to persuade the payor to make an offer that larger percentages of physicians have preauthorized.

  Legality: According to DOJ and FTC personnel, this is illegal price fixing because the messenger is negotiating with the payor. The messenger cannot act as the negotiating agent of the physicians.

- **Variation:** Same facts as above, except that instead of using preauthorized fee ranges, the physicians decide that the messenger should negotiate an agreement with the payor. To avoid the bar on price fixing, the "negative option" is used—the negotiated agreement is relayed back to each physician individually for acceptance or rejection. Each physician is deemed to have accepted the offer unless the physician affirmatively states that the physician does not want to be included.

  Legality: This arrangement is illegal. The messenger comes too close to negotiating an agreement on behalf of all of the physicians. Statement 9 says that use of the negative option is not necessarily enough to save an otherwise illegal arrangement. Use of the negative option may be legal if the messenger does not engage in any negotiations with the payor after presenting the price information from the physicians. In that context, the negative option may be a way to reduce the expense of this model.

- **Variation:** Same facts as above except that 65% of the physicians in the community plan to be in the arrangement.

Legality: As discussed above with regard to size limits, it is uncertain whether this will be legal. The DOJ/FTC become uncomfortable when large percentages of physicians in a market are part of the same cooperative arrangement. However, when the messenger model is used, technically there is no agreement restraining trade among the physicians. The only thing that can be said with certainty is that as percentages increase, the DOJ/FTC are more likely to investigate.

Non-integrated Network that Presents and Discusses Non-fee Related Information and Uses the Messenger Model for Financial Arrangements

Please note: These scenarios and determinations of legality are verbatim from Frequently Asked Questions provided by the DOJ/FTC. They are presented as informational and do not constitute legal or professional advice. Antitrust laws are always decided on case specifics.

Case Scenario The physicians in solo and small group practice in a community, which constitute 45% of the physicians, decide to organize a network to contract with managed-care plans. The physicians want the network for four reasons. First, they are concerned about losing patients and they want to contract with managed-care plans in order to gain patient referrals. They are willing to discount fees in return for referrals. Second, the market has become very competitive and new forms of payment have entered the market. In order to know whether offers they make will be competitive or not, the physicians want to take a survey of fee levels and other fee related terms that are prevalent in the market. Third, they want to have influence over the medical policy of the plans, as they are concerned about the quality of care that results from the medical policies of some of the plans. Fourth, they want to have input into health plans about administrative matters that affect their practices, such as, preauthorization procedures and patient grievance procedures.

To take a survey, the physicians will have a county medical society perform a survey of fees charged by physicians in the market and a survey of other matters, such as medical policy and administrative procedures used by health plans. The surveyor will get information from more than five physicians, and will aggregate the information in such a way that no one physician accounts for more than 25% of the content of any one statistic on an average weighted basis, and it is not possible to discern the charges of any given physician in the market. After aggregation, the messenger will share data that is at least three months old with the physicians. The physicians will consider that data when deciding on discounts.

To make financial arrangements with payors, the physicians plan to have a healthcare consultant or an executive from their county medical society act a messenger. Each physician will communicate with the messenger individually and authorize the messenger to accept contracts that fall within a fee range. The physicians will not communicate with each other about fees, and the messenger will not share the fee information with the physicians. The messenger will create two schedules. One will show the results of the survey of fees prevalent in the market. The other will show the percentage of physicians in the network willing to accept various fee levels, and will accept contract offers made by payors, that fall within the fee range of any physician or which are better. Offers lower than the fee range of any physician will be forwarded to the physician for acceptance or rejection. However, the messenger will not negotiate with or jawbone the payor.

The physicians in the network will also appoint a committee to consider the medical policies or the plans that they contract with. The committee members will solicit concerns or complaints about any contracting payor's medical policy, and they will also refer to the survey of medical policy taken by the medical society. The committee will then consider whether to recommend changes in policy to a payor. The committee may obtain information about the medical issue involved from literature, and may draft recommended protocols. If the committee decides that there should be a change, it will then present the information to the payor in question and attempt to persuade the payor to change its medical policy and adopt a protocol recommended by the committee. However, the committee will not threaten to boycott the plan if it does not adopt its recommendations, nor will it implement a boycott.

The physicians will also form a committee to consider the administrative procedures of the plan that they contract with. They will solicit concerns and complaints from the physicians in the network about administrative procedures of the plans, they will consider the survey of procedures taken by the medical society, and will consider ways that the procedures could be improved. The committee will then meet with the health plan management to discuss its recommendations and attempt to persuade them to adopt them. However, the committee will not threaten a boycott or implement a boycott.

Legality This arrangement is legal. The messenger model meets the criteria of Statement 9. The collective provision and discussion of medical data falls within the safety zone of Statement 4 of the 1996 guidelines, and the collection and exchange of fee information is in Statements 5 and 6. The collective discussion of administrative matters would be analyzed under the rule of reason, but meets the criteria of Statement 4.

- **Variation on the Arrangement**: 75% of the physicians in the community will be in the network.

  Legality: According to the DOJ/FTC, the guidelines do not comment on network size for the messenger model. It appears that since there is no agreement, that it can be very large. However, once the network starts assuming other functions, such as agreeing on medical policy and administrative policy and trying to persuade plans to accept those policies, then it starts to look more like a joint venture that is subject to size limits. But, the network described may not have market power even if 75% of the physicians participate, because it does no more than have dialogues with plans and attempt to persuade them to adopt policies.

- **Variation on the Arrangement**: A payor reviews the information submitted, and then submits an offer that is lower than the messenger has authority to accept for more than 15% of the network physicians. The messenger objects, points out that the offer made is well below fee levels currently prevailing in the market, and tries to get the payor to make an offer that the messenger can accept on behalf of at least 75% of the physicians. The messenger points out that this level is below the average fee level prevailing in the market. To support the case for higher fees, the messenger points out that the payor can have a network right away, but the messenger will have to send lower fee offers back to the physicians for individual consideration and find out which ones may be willing to accept it, a process that could take several weeks. At the end of that time, it might be that not many would have accepted, so the payor and the messenger would have to start over again, taking still more time.

  Legality: According to the DOJ/FTC, this is clearly illegal. The messenger is negotiating with the payor.

Regrettably, both the creation and the operation of some provider networks raise the risk of violating both federal and state antitrust laws. Healthcare providers have been the subject of recent antitrust enforcement agencies activities by both federal and state agencies. It is thus incumbent upon healthcare providers to analyze carefully the structure and operation of a provider network to minimize their potential antitrust risk.

A recent innovation in network structure, which may help healthcare providers to compete more effectively in the managed-care environment, is *the qualified managed care plan (QMCP)*.

First announced in 1995 by the Antitrust Division of the Department of Justice (DOJ) and the Connecticut Attorney General in consent decrees entered into with PHOs, and their IPAs, a QMCP has also been proposed as a form of resolution as recently as April 1997 in a DOJ action against a Louisiana hospital and its PHO.

A QMCP may provide physician networks with considerable flexibility in achieving compliance with the antitrust laws and may also be adaptable to many other types of provider organizations.

How the QMCP Concept Came About?

The 1994 Statements of Antitrust Enforcement Policy and Analytical Principles Relating to Health Care and Antitrust (the guidelines), issued jointly by the DOJ and the Federal Trade Commission (FTC), outline the methodology utilized by the federal antitrust enforcers to evaluate, among other functions, compliance by a provider network with the federal antitrust laws. Physician networks that meet the requirements of the "safety zone" contained within Statement 8 of the guidelines will not be challenged "absent extraordinary circumstances." These requirements are as follows:

- The network, if exclusive, must include no more than 20% of the physicians in a specialty in the relevant geographic market (30% in the network is nonexclusive); and
- The network's physicians must share substantial financial risk as a group, either through capitation or financial withholds based on preset cost containment goals.

Simply put, a network's market share and the degree to which its members are economically integrated through shared financial risk are critical to an assessment of a network's antitrust exposure.

In many previously adjudicated antitrust cases, PHOs were alleged to have set fee schedules and negotiated collectively on behalf of their members even though those members did share substantial financial risk and/or to have contained a far greater number of physicians than permitted by the safety zone.

A QMCP may also be an appropriate vehicle for other types of provider networks (for example, networks of healthcare institutions or individual practitioners other than physicians). Since the QMCP has only been applied to physician networks, however, other types of networks must be carefully analyzed on a case-by-case basis.

Participants who share substantial financial risk through a QMCP have considerable flexibility when setting fees and negotiating with payors for network contracts, but should exercise caution to avoid allegations of illegal price-fixing for services to out-of-network patients.

A provider network that operates on a non-risk-sharing basis (for example, contracts on a fee-for-service basis without withholds with some or all payors) must, in accordance with the guidelines, use a "messenger model." Under this approach, neither the network nor the messenger may negotiate collectively for the provider members with respect to fees and "other competitive terms and conditions" of managed-care contracts.

Federal antitrust enforcement officials have recently stated that they may release revisions to the guidelines sometime during the summer of 1997. The agencies are considering other acceptable types and levels of shared financial risk, less restrictive messenger models, and other methods by which to permit provider networks to operate with a greater degree of flexibility in this rapidly changing marketplace.

Qualified in the term QMCP means qualified only with respect to antitrust concerns. Other equally important legal issues, well beyond my scope as a paralegal, may be involved in the structuring and operating of a provider network, including Medicare/Medicaid fraud and abuse, Stark anti-self referral provisions, Medicare/Medicaid Physician Incentive Plan rules, tax exemption and corporate formation issues, corporate practice of medicine limitations, employee and ERISA issues, utilization review, licensure and liability (in Texas), and corporate governance. Always check with professional counsel with expertise in health law.

A distinction has been made between "exclusive" and "nonexclusive" physician network joint ventures. In an "exclusive" venture, the network's physician participants are restricted from individually contracting or affiliating with other network joint ventures or health plans. In a "nonexclusive" venture, the physician participants are available to affiliate with other networks or contract individually with health plans.

Factors which the agencies will examine on the question of nonexclusivity include the following:

a) That viable competing networks or managed-care plans with adequate physician participation currently exist in the market;

b) That physicians in the network actually individually participate in, or contract with, other networks or managed-care plans, or there is other evidence of their willingness and incentive to do so;

c) That physicians in the network earn substantial revenue from other networks or through individual contracts with managed-care plans;

d) The absence of any indications of significant de-participation from other networks or managed-care plans in the market; and

e) The absence of any indications of coordination among the physicians in the network regarding price or other competitively significant terms of participation in other networks or managed-care plans.

If contract provisions significantly restrict the ability or willingness of network physicians to join other networks or contract individually with managed-care plans, the agencies will consider the network to be exclusive for the purposes of antitrust "safety zone."

Substantial Financial Risk Must be Shared   To qualify for either the exclusive or nonexclusive physician network joint venture antitrust "safety zone", the participants in a physician network joint venture must share substantial financial risk in providing all the services that are jointly priced through the network. Examples of some types of arrangements through which participants in a physician network joint venture can share substantial financial risk, include the following:

(a) Agreement by the venture to provide services to a health plan at a "capitated" rate;

(b) Agreement by the venture to provide designated services or classes of services to a health plan for a predetermined percentage of premium or revenue from the plan;

(c) Use by the venture of significant financial incentives for its physician participants, as a group, to achieve specified cost-containment goals. For example, two methods by which the venture can accomplish this are:

   (i) Withholding from all physician participants in the network a substantial amount of the compensation due to them, with distribution of that amount to the physician participants based on group performance in meeting the cost-containment goals of the network as a whole; or

   (ii) Establishing overall cost or utilization targets for the network as a whole, with the network's physician participants subject to subsequent substantial financial rewards or penalties based on group performance in meeting the targets.

(d) Agreement by the venture to provide a complex or extended course of treatment that requires the substantial coordination of care by physicians in different specialties offering a complementary mix of services, for a fixed, predetermined payment, where the costs of that course of treatment for any individual patient can vary greatly due to the individual patient's condition, the choice, complexity, length of treatment, or other factors.

Inasmuch as new risk sharing arrangements are constantly emerging in this changing healthcare marketplace, those creating physician network joint ventures can also take advantage of the Department of Justice's expedited business review procedure or the FTC's advisory opinion procedure.

Agency Analysis of Physician Network Joint Ventures that Fall Outside of these Antitrust "Safety Zones"   Physician network joint ventures that fall outside of the antitrust "safety zones" do not necessarily raise substantial antitrust concerns. Likewise, those joint ventures that do not involve the sharing of substantial financial risk may also be viewed as noncompetitive. It is not the agencies' intent to treat physician networks either more strictly or more leniently than joint ventures in any other industry. Instead, the agencies' goal is to ensure a competitive marketplace in which consumers will have the benefit of high quality, cost-effective healthcare and a wide range of choices, including new provider-controlled networks that expand consumer choice and increase competition.

Therefore, where competitors economically integrate in a joint venture, such agreements, if reasonably necessary to accomplish the pro-competitive benefits of the integration, are analyzed under the "rule of reason" analysis. The agencies will basically apply the following type of evaluation (Note, however, that the agencies' ultimate conclusion is based upon a more comprehensive analysis.):

1) They will define the relevant market;
2) They will evaluate the competitive effects of the physician joint venture;
3) They will evaluate the impact of pro-competitive efficiencies which result from this joint venture; and
4) They will evaluate collateral agreements or conditions that unreasonably restrict competition and are unlikely to contribute significantly to the legitimate purpose of the physician network joint venture.

In this policy statement, the agencies provide seven examples of physician joint ventures, and subject them to "rule of reason" analysis. As a paralegal, I am not licensed to be able to provide specific advice as to whether your integrated network joint ventures are in compliance with Federal antitrust law and these guidelines. Every joint venture is unique and the application of the antitrust laws can be quite complex. Retaining legal counsel is essential if you are considering entering into, or creating an integrated network joint venture.

Statement 9—Multi-provider Networks
Healthcare providers are forming a wide range of new relationships and affiliations, including networks among otherwise competing providers, as well as networks of providers offering complementary or unrelated services. Because multi-provider networks involve a large variety of structures and relationships among many different types of healthcare providers, and new arrangements are continually developing, the agencies are

unable to establish a meaningful antitrust "safety zone" for any of these arrangements.

As stated previously, the antitrust laws condemn as per se illegal naked arrangements among competitors that fix prices or allocate markets. However, a "rule of reason" analysis will be applied and the network will not be viewed as per se illegal, if the providers' integration through the network is likely to produce significant efficiencies that benefit consumers, and any price agreements (or other agreements that would otherwise be per se illegal) by the network providers are reasonably necessary to realize those efficiencies.

Shared Substantial Financial Risk In some multi-provider networks, significant efficiencies may be achieved through agreement by the competing providers to share substantial financial risk for the services provided through the network. In such cases, the setting of price would be integral to the network's use of such an arrangement, and therefore, would warrant evaluation under "rule of reason." Examples of substantial financial risks can be found in Section 8 of this fact-sheet. Organizers of multi-provider networks who are uncertain whether their proposed arrangements constitute substantial financial risk sharing can also take advantage of the Department of Justice's expedited business review procedure or the FTC's advisory opinion procedure.

No Sharing of Financial Risk Multi-provider networks that do not involve the sharing of substantial financial risk may also be sufficiently integrated to demonstrate that the venture is likely to produce significant efficiencies. These arrangements will also be analyzed under "rule of reason."

"Rule of Reason" Analysis In "rule of reason" analysis of multi-provider networks, the agencies will basically apply the following type of evaluation (Note, however, that the agencies' ultimate conclusion is based upon a more comprehensive analysis.):

1) They will evaluate the competitive effects of multi-provider networks in each of the relevant markets in which these networks operate or have substantial impact.

The relevant geographic market for each relevant product market affected by the multi-provider network will be determined through a fact-specific analysis that focuses on the location of reasonable alternatives. Therefore, the relevant geographic market may be broader for some product markets than for others;

2) They will examine the competitive effects of the network, both the potential "horizontal" and "vertical" effects of the arrangement, and its exclusion of particular providers; and

3) The agencies will review the balance of any potential anti-competitive effects of the multi-provider network against potential efficiencies associated with its formation and operation. The greater the network's likely anti-competitive effects, the greater must be the network's likely efficiencies.

In conducting a "rule of reason" analysis, the agencies rely upon a wide variety of data and information, including information supplied by the participants in the multi-provider network, purchasers, providers, consumers, and others familiar with the market in question. It is not simply a question of polling those who support and oppose the formation of the network. Some common arrangements include:

Selective Contracting Exclusion of particular providers may be a method by which networks limit provider plans in an effort to achieve quality and cost-containment goals, and thus enhance their ability to compete against other networks. Selective contracting may also be pro-competitive by giving nonparticipant providers an incentive to form competing networks. A "rule of reason" analysis will again be applied. In examining exclusive arrangements, the agencies will examine the degree to which the arrangements may limit the ability of other networks or health plans to compete in the market. The focus of the analysis is not on whether a particular provider has been harmed by the exclusion or referral policies, but rather whether the conduct reduces competition among providers in the market and thereby harms consumers.

Messenger Models   Some networks that are not substantially integrated use a variety of "messenger model" arrangements to facilitate non-integrated network contracting and avoid price-fixing agreements among competing network providers. Arrangements that are designed simply to minimize the costs associated with the contracting process that do not result in a collective determination by the competing network's providers on prices or price-related terms, are not per se illegal price fixing.

The key issue in any messenger model arrangement is whether the arrangement creates or facilitates an agreement among competitors on prices or price-related terms. Determining whether there is such an agreement is a question of fact in each case. The agencies will examine whether the agent facilitates collective decision-making by network providers, rather than independent, unilateral decisions. In particular, the agencies will examine whether the agent coordinates the providers' responses to a particular proposal, disseminates to network providers the views or intentions of other network providers as to the proposal, expresses an opinion on the terms offered, collectively negotiates for the providers, or decides whether or not to convey an offer based on the agent's judgment about the attractiveness of the prices or price-related terms. If the agent engages in such activities, the arrangement may amount to a per se illegal price-fixing agreement.

In this policy statement, the agencies provide four examples of multi-provider network joint ventures, and subjected them to antitrust analysis. As a paralegal, I cannot provide specific legal advice as to whether your multi-provider networks are in compliance with federal antitrust law and these guidelines. Every multi-provider network joint venture is unique and the application of the antitrust laws can be quite complex. Retaining legal counsel is essential if you are considering entering into, participating in, or creating a multi-provider network joint venture.

Useful Addresses and Telephone Numbers

To contact the Antitrust Division regarding business review letters, call or write the agency at:

Legal Procedure Unit
Antitrust Division
U.S. Department of Justice
325 7th Street, N. W.
Suite 215
Washington, D. C. 20530
Telephone number: (202) 514-2481

To contact the Federal Trade Commission regarding advisory opinions, call or write the agency at:

Health Care Division
Bureau of Competition
Federal Trade Commission
Washington, D. C. 25080
Telephone number: (202) 326-2756

NOTE: **This chapter is designed to provide general information about the antitrust laws, and the Department of Justice and Federal Trade Commission's guidelines on antitrust enforcement policy in healthcare. The memorandum does not constitute specific legal advice nor does it represent an official position for Maria K. Todd, HealthPro Consulting Consortium, Inc. or McGraw-Hill as the publisher. For specific questions about the contents in this memorandum, please contact your local healthcare attorney.**

10
CHAPTER

Business Plan
Development

As an IPA, PHO, or MSO, it will be necessary to state your business goals, objectives, and projections in words for others to be able to read and evaluate. One of the best business plan tools I have found in the software market is *Jian's Biz Plan Builder Interactive.* It creates a simple to use template for business plan development. They have the headlines, sentences developed, and model paragraphs. Then as you develop your document the wizards have spaces to fill in the blanks with most of the opportunities supported by an example of the text to serve as a guide or idea.

The document builder comes in several sections allowing you to decide upon your finished look as a group, make necessary changes, and then print the finished document. By using the software, I have created for you a sample summary report for a fictitious HealthPro IPA, LLC. As you read through the next few pages, think of how you might fill in the blanks for your organization. Also, obtain the guide to business plan development *Business Plan for Small Service Firms Management* Aids-2.022, available for a nominal fee from your local Small Business Administration.

Below is the first step, deciding what to put into your business plan and having a direction. Break each part into a standard essay format with a Thesis statement and introductory paragraph or two, a few supporting paragraphs, and a conclusion. An example that is most popular with startups follows:

Table of Contents

Executive Summary

Financial Plan

Assumptions

Financial Statements

Capital Requirements

Use of Funds

Exit/Payback Strategy

Conclusion

For the sake of demonstration, I have abbreviated the business plan to simply give you an idea of how the document flows. Normally, business plans are very formal documents with much elaboration on the areas I have highlighted. What I have found out is that your investor or banker wants to see a well-designed plan, with a viable rationale, and lots of substance instead of "fluff."

THE EXECUTIVE SUMMARY

This section provides several parts, namely, Company Direction, Company Overview, (background, objectives, and capital requirements), Management Team, Service Strategy, Market Analysis, Customer Profile, Marketing Plan, Marketing Strategy, Advertising and Promotion, Public Relations, Financial Plan, and Conclusion. Following is a sample of HealthPro IPA, LLC's Executive Summary.

Company Direction

In 1997, HealthPro IPA, LLC was founded to form an organization of healthcare providers that could exercise some contracting clout with managed-care payors, share risk, preserve clinical autonomy and access to patients, and promote professional camaraderie between providers in the community while delivering quality healthcare at an affordable price.

Overall, our company can be characterized as a high profile, aggressive, healthcare provider organization known for its quality care and business leadership in the community.

Company Overview

Background—For many years, providers have contracted directly with insurance plans, HMOs, PPOs, and others, often at a disadvantage, without the leverage needed to negotiate from a position of strength.

The condition of the industry today is such that managed healthcare plans are deferring the network development activities to organized groups of providers ready to share risk with them.

The legal form of HealthPro IPA, LLC is Limited Liability Company. We chose the Limited Liability Company form because of the inherent flexibility of size and tax advantages.

HealthPro IPA, LLC's business headquarters is located at 1562 South Parker Road, Denver, CO, United States, 80231-2719.

Revenue projected for fiscal year [current fiscal year] without external funding is expected to be [current internal revenue dollars]. Annual growth is projected to be [annual growth percent] through [growth ending year].

Now, HealthPro IPA, LLC is at a point where [future needs/wants].

Objectives—Based on our projected revenues for the current fiscal year and our projected annual growth, we feel that within [time span] years HealthPro IPA, LLC will be in a suitable position for [future company position]. Our objective, at this time, is to propel the company into a prominent market position.

Capital Requirements—According to the opportunities and requirements for HealthPro IPA, LLC described in this business plan, and based on what we feel are sound business assumptions, our [capital time frame] capital requirements are for [capital required dollars].

To accomplish this goal we have developed a comprehensive plan to intensify and accelerate our marketing and sales activities, services expansion, and customer service. To implement our plans we require an estimated total of [5 year loan dollars] in financing over the next five years for the following purposes:

[fund use]

We require additional investments of [additional capital dollars and time frame] in order to increase our production capacities to meet market demand.

Management Team

Our management team consists of six men and women:

Dr. Harry Jones, M.D., President and CEO
Dr. Susan James, Vice President
Punjit Ala, M.D., Secretary
Sandra Allan, D.O., Treasurer
Raul Martinez, M.D., Medical Director
Mohammed Khaldi, M.D., Director of Operations

Their backgrounds consist of more than [overall experience] years of experience. Our CEO and advisory staff have a total of [corporate development experience] years of managed-care experience and IPA participation.

Additionally, our outside management advisors provide tremendous support for management decisions and creativity.

[outside support name and title]

Service Strategy

Current Service Medical and Surgical services to managed-care participants, Medicare and Medicaid patients and others with and without private health insurance coverage.

Caring for our patients is our primary focus.

Market Analysis

Market Definition—The managed-care delivery system market is growing at a rapid rate. The market for HMO growth amounted to [market dollars] in [market year]. This represents [market growth percent] growth over the last [previous market years] years.

According to market research and industry sources, the overall [market type] market for the [industry type] industry is projected to be [market dollars for industry] by the end of [market industry year]. The area of greatest growth in the managed-care market is in the area of provider risk assumption and capitation. Currently, the market is shared by [market participants], with [top competitor] considered the market leader.

Customer Profile

HealthPro IPA, LLC's target market includes manage-care insurance and health plans, HMOs, PPOs, EPOs, healthcare purchasing coalitions and alliances, ERISA self-funded health plans, and other emerging groups. The most typical customer for our services are managed healthcare plans, and who currently uses our product for quality healthcare delivery and cost containment.

A partial list of actual customers includes:

[customer list]

Competition—Companies that compete in this market are [key competitors]. All companies mentioned charge competitive prices as follows:

[competitor products and prices].

Key factors that have resulted in the present competitive position in this industry are [key competitive factors].

In all comparisons, HealthPro IPA, LLC's provides superior performance than do competitive organizations because of our well-developed organizational infrastructure and our ability to share substantial risk among all members. In most cases, the number of differences is substantial. A complete technical comparison is available.

HealthPro IPA, LLC's network can participate in virtually all situations involved with managed health delivery. The ability to be flexible to the needs of the customer with full capability on utilization management, quality improvement, and severity adjusted, acuity indexed outcomes is unique to HealthPro IPA, LLC's network. The ability to demonstrate this using our own data is unique to our network, and our research indicates its performance is superior to anything else in our market today.

Risk—The top business risks that HealthPro IPA, LLC faces are [top business risks].

The economic risks affecting HealthPro IPA, LLC are [economic risks].

Marketing Plan

Responses from customers indicate that our network is enjoying an excellent reputation and we fully intend to continue this trend. Inquiries from prospective customers suggest that there is considerable demand for it.

HealthPro IPA, LLC's marketing strategy is to enhance, promote, and support the fact that our products [product marketing strategy].

Marketing Strategy

Because of the special market characteristics [special market characteristics], our strategy includes [sales strategy].

Advertising and Promotion

HealthPro IPA, LLC's overall advertising and promotional objectives are to position HealthPro IPA, LLC as the leader in the market.

We will develop an advertising campaign built around [ad campaign message], beginning with a "who we are" statement and supporting it with ads that reinforce this message. Additionally, we will develop a consistent reach and frequency throughout the year. In addition to standard advertising practices, we will gain considerable recognition through [other advertising practices].

For the next year, advertising and promotion will require [advertising money needs]. On an ongoing basis we will budget our advertising investment as 3% of gross revenues.

Public Relations

During [publicity strategy year], HealthPro IPA, LLC will focus on the following publicity strategies:

[top publicity strategies]

We will track, wherever possible, the incremental revenue generated from our advertising, promotion, and publicity efforts. We anticipate at least [publicity sales dollars] of sales will be generated directly from our publicity, and possibly additional [indirect dollar increase in sales] of indirect increase in sales throughout our various channels.

Financial Plan

The financial projections indicate that profit will be achievable in 2 years. The increase in profits generated by this investment, specifically [expected increase description] will allow us to have the funds to develop a Management Services Organization (MSO) in the next 18 months.

Conclusion

HealthPro IPA, LLC enjoys an established track-record of excellence with our customers. Their expressions of satisfaction and encouragement are numerous, and we intend to continue our advances and growth in the marketplace with more unique and effective products.

[Executive Summary Concluding Remarks]

FINANCIAL PLAN

Here is a great opportunity to enlist the assistance of the network's finance committee. A PHO may have an easier time if the finance committee and the hospital's CFO participate in the development of these documents, but IPAs that have some participant interested in finance and numbers usually do very well with this section.

First we start with a section of assumptions about when the network will be up and running and how long it will take to reach profitability and projected market penetration. Then following is a section that actually projects some numbers for total revenue, gross profit, and income from operations, followed by income ratios, gross profit analysis, a budget with income statements, balance sheets, and cash flow statements.

The reader is going to be curious about how the money will be used and how you intend to service your debt and offer exit strategies to those who may leave the organization. Be sure to include these statements and be honest and forthright. If you do not have an answer, seek professional assistance for these answers from an experienced financial consultant.

ASSUMPTIONS

Our financial projections are based on the following assumptions:

A working network will be available by [working prototype date].

Initial market penetration is anticipated to be [market penetration dollars] at a margin of [market penetration margin percent]. This is expected to increase to [year 1 increase market penetration dollars] by the end of Year 1 and to [year 5 increase market penetration dollars] by the end of Year 5.

Gross Profit Analysis

The Gross Profit Analysis statements included in our supporting documents show monthly sales revenue, cost of goods sold, and gross profit values for each of our service lines for the first year.

Financial Statements Primary Income—Related Items

Year	Fiscal Year 1	Fiscal Year 2	Fiscal Year 3	Fiscal Year 4	Fiscal Year 5
Total revenue	$383,077	$586,531	$795,576	$1,024,167	$1,245,676
Growth, %		53%	36%	29%	22%
Gross profit	−$105,165	$123,183	$228,614	$343,739	$452,601
Growth, %		−217%	86%	50%	32%
Income from operations	−$232,660	−$28,550	$38,211	$99,881	$163,696
Growth, %		−88%	−234%	161%	64%
Net income after taxes	− $244,094	$39,542	$24,497	$71,111	$111,474
Growth, %		−84%	−162%	190%	57%

Income Ratios

Year	Fiscal Year 1	Fiscal Year 2	Fiscal Year 3	Fiscal Year 4	Fiscal Year 5
Gross profit margin	−27%	21%	29%	34%	36%
Operating income margin	−61%	−5%	5%	10%	13%
Net profit margin	−64%	− 7%	3%	7%	9%
Return on equity	0%	0%	0%	0%	0%

Budget—Income Statements

There are three income statements included in our supporting documents:

- Year 1 by month
- Years 2-3 by quarter
- Years 1-5

Balance Sheets

There are three balance sheets included in our supporting documents:

- Year 1 by month
- Years 2-3 by quarter
- Years 1-5

Cash Flows Statements

There are three statements of changes in financial position (Cash Flows Statements) included in our supporting documents:

- Year 1 by month
- Years 2-3 by quarter
- Years 1-5

Break-Even Analysis

The break-even analysis included in our supporting documents indicates that the break-even point will be reached in [break-even month and year].

Revenue is projected to be [dollars above break-even] above break-even in [revenue above break-even month and year].

The contribution margin for the first year is 59%, which represents a break-even sales volume of $179,097, and a sales volume above break-even of $50,356.

CAPITAL REQUIREMENTS

The [capital time frame] capital required is [capital required dollars]. We require additional investments of [additional capital dollars and time frame] in order to increase our production capacities to meet market demand.

After analyzing our working capital, we estimate our operating working capital requirements as [year 1 working capital], [year 2 working capital], [year 3 working capital], [year 4 working capital], and [year 5 working capital] for years one through five, respectively. We will need to borrow [working capital finance dollars] to finance working capital for a period of [working capital finance time frame]. The remainder will be financed through cash from operations.

In order to purchase [purchase additions], an estimated total of [5 year loan dollars] in financing is required for the next five-year period. The annual requirements for each year are estimated as [year 1 loan dollars], [year 2 loan dollars], [year 3 loan dollars], [year 4 loan dollars], and [year 5 loan dollars] respectively.

The level of safety is [safety level] for this [industry or investment type]. Our confidence in achieving the attached financial projections within [achievement percent] is [confidence level]. In addition to the operation of the business, additional protection is provided by [protector] as collateral. Were the situation to arise where the collateral was needed, the realizable value of the collateral would be [collateral value dollars], which reduces the amount "at risk" to [at risk dollars]. With a projected return of [projected return dollars], this represents a return of [at risk return percent] of the amount at risk.

USE OF FUNDS

The funding proceeds will be used to [fund use].

EXIT/PAYBACK STRATEGY

The financial projections indicate that exit of [investor name] will be achievable in [years investor exit] years. The exit settlement will be in the form of [investor exit strategy]. The increase in profits generated by this investment, specifically [expected increase description] will allow us to have the funds to repay the loan in [payback time frame].

CONCLUSION

HealthPro IPA, LLC enjoys an established track-record of excellence with our customers. Their expressions of satisfaction and encouragement are numerous, and we intend to continue our advances and growth in the marketplace with more unique and effective products.

Based on the attached financial projections, we believe that this venture represents a sound business investment.

In order to [business progression] we are requesting a [financing type] of [financing amount] by [financing date].

[end sample document]

A business plan need not be a hindrance, so try not to become too bogged down in specifics that you cannot be flexible as a company to meet market changes without starting the plan over from scratch. Some additional information sources are included below in case you want to do more research in this area.

RESOURCES

Federal Government Resources

Bureau of the Census
Issues publications covering demographic and economic surveys. These are often available for review at any government depository library.

Bureau of the Budget
Standard Industrial Classification Manual: A publication that lists the SIC numbers issued to major areas of business.

Department of Commerce

Census of Business
Retail Area Statistics Census Tract Manual County and City Data Book. This book is updated every three years and contains statistical information on population, education, employment, income, housing, and retail sales.

County Business Patterns Directory of Federal Statistics for Local Areas Facts for Marketers Measuring Markets: A guide to the use of federal and state statistical data.

Small Business Administration
SBA Small Business Answer Desk (1-800-368-5855)

National Directories for use in marketing, small marketers aids and statistics and maps for market analysis.

Books

Handbook for Raising Capital: Financing Alternatives for Emerging and Growing Businesses, by Lawrence Chimerine, Robert F. Cushman, and Howard D. Ross.

The Ernst and Young Guide to Raising Capital, by R. Owen and R. Conway.

Business Plan Checklist—Business Planning Diagnostics, by Coopers and Lybrand.

Business Plans to Manage Day-to-Day Operations, by Christopher R. Malburg.

KEEPING YOUR INFANT BUSINESS COMPETITIVE— NON-DISCLOSURE AGREEMENTS

Following the design of your business plan, you will need to protect your interests as best as possible. You can start with a non-disclosure statement for those who you allow to read the plan, so that you have not given them the cookbook to build a competitive organization as a clone to yours. The following non-disclosure statement model may help you:

SAMPLE NON-DISCLOSURE AGREEMENT

NON-DISCLOSURE AGREEMENT

The undersigned acknowledges that HealthPro Independent Physicians' Association has furnished to the undersigned potential Investor ("Investor") certain proprietary data ("Confidential Information") relating to the business affairs and operations of HealthPro Independent Physicians' Association for study and evaluation by Investor for possibly investing in HealthPro Independent Physicians' Association.

NON-DISCLOSURE AGREEMENT—Concluded

It is acknowledged by Investor that the information provided by HealthPro Independent Physicians' Association is confidential, therefore, Investor agrees not to disclose it and not to disclose that any discussions or contracts with HealthPro Independent Physicians' Association have occurred or are intended, other than as provided for in the following paragraph.

It is acknowledged by Investor that information to be furnished is in all respects confidential in nature, other than information which is in the public domain through other means and that any disclosure or use of same by Investor, except as provided in this agreement, may cause serious harm or damage to HealthPro Independent Physicians' Association and its owners and officers. Therefore, Investor agrees that Investor will not use the information furnished for any purpose other than as stated above, and agrees that Investor will not either directly or indirectly by agent, employee, or representative, disclose this information, either in whole or in part, to any third party, provided, however that (a) information furnished may be disclosed only to those directors, officers, and employees of Investor and to Investor's advisors or their representatives who need such information for the purpose of evaluating any possible transaction (it being understood that those directors, officers, employees, advisors and representatives shall be informed by Investor of the confidential nature of such information and shall be directed by Investor to treat such information confidentially), and (b) any disclosure of information may be made to which HealthPro Independent Physicians' Association consents in writing. At the close of negotiations, Investor will return to HealthPro Independent Physicians' Association all records, reports, documents, and memoranda furnished and will not make or retain any copy thereof.

_____   _____
           Signature   Date

_____
Name (typed or printed)
[Addressee Company]

This is a business plan. It does not imply an offering of securities.

Remember, to Fail to Plan is to Plan to Fail!

11
CHAPTER

Capitation Performance Guarantees

Managed-care agreements for IPAs, PHOs, MSOs, and PPMs are ever increasingly being signed as full-risk, percentage of premium, capitated contracts. When an HMO signs an agreement with one of these groups, the capitation paid is likely to be a large sum of money each month. Therefore, contracts and agreements of this type involve heavy liability on the part of the HMO to do the necessary due diligence with the organization with regards to economic credentialing. The last thing that an HMO wants to receive is a "Dear John" letter from the provider network comptroller postmarked from some far off island that says: "Dear Mr. HMO-CEO, We quit. Sincerely, The IPA."

Hence, many managed-care agreements contain specific performance language with regards to the provision of covered services and the groups performance. In this short chapter, I would like to share with you some model language from contracts I have reviewed in the past so that *when* you see them, you will not become unnecessarily surprised. Often the body of the contract includes a Guarantee of Provision of Covered Services:

"IPA shall establish a plan that ensures the provision and continuation of Covered Service Participants for which capitation

payments have been made, and the provision and continuation of Covered Services to Participants who are confined in an inpatient facility until their discharge or expiration of covered services, in the event of group's failure to provide or continue such covered services whether such failure results from a breach of this agreement by the group, the insolvency of the group or otherwise. The plan must be in all respects acceptable to payor in its sole and absolute discretion and may include, (a) sufficient insurance to cover the expenses to be paid for such covered services; (b) provisions in provider contracts that obligate the provider to provide medically necessary covered services for the duration of the period for which capitation payments have been paid to the group and until the participant's discharge from inpatient facilities; (c) reserves in amounts sufficient to cover expenses to be paid for such medically necessary covered services; (d) letters of credit in amounts sufficient to cover expenses to be paid for such medically necessary covered services; and (e) such other arrangements that assure that the medically necessary covered services described above are provided to participants.

The group shall submit its initial plan for this guarantee of covered services to payor for its approval at least twenty (20) business days prior to the effective date of this agreement. Thereafter, the plan may not be changed in any respect without the prior written consent of the payor."

Additionally, another part of the contract or agreement is going to ask for a Guarantee of the Group's Performance:

"Prior to the effective date of this agreement, the group shall notify the payor in writing of the persons or entities that (a) are shareholders or partners of the group, (b) control any of the shareholders or partners of the group, (c) have a significant influence on the management of the group, or (d) have a significant economic interest in the group. The payor shall promptly notify the group of those persons or entities that payor desires to have guarantee the group's performance under this agreement. Group shall cause each of such persons or entities identified by payor to execute a Guarantee of Performance in favor of payor in the form of the Guarantee of Performance set forth in Exhibit A.

If there is any change in the persons or entities described in the above paragraph, the group shall immediately notify payor of such change and shall cause any additional persons or entities satisfying the criteria described above to execute Guarantee of Performance if requested by payor."

Exhibit A—Capitation Guarantee of Performance: This Guarantee of Performance is entered into as of _____ ____, 19____, (this "Guarantee") by John Smith, M.D. , a partner in Gulf Shore Medical Associates, IPA, L.L.C., a limited liability corporation incorporated under the laws of the state of Florida ("Guarantor") in favor of Gulf Coast HMO of Florida, Inc., ("Payor") and its affiliates in connection with the Group Agreement (the "Agreement") between Gulf Coast HMO of Florida, Inc., and Gulf Shore Medical Associates, IPA, L.L.C.

WHEREAS, Guarantor is [a partner] [a shareholder] [describe other relationship to group] that will benefit substantially and significantly from group entering into the agreement with payor.

WHEREAS, as a condition of entering into the Agreement with Group or as a condition of continuing the Agreement with Group, payor has required that Guarantor execute this guarantee in favor of payor and its affiliates.

NOW, THEREFORE, for good and valuable consideration, the receipt and sufficiency are hereby acknowledged, Guarantor hereby agrees as follows:

1. Guarantee: Guarantor hereby unconditionally and irrevocably guarantees the full, complete, and punctual financial performance of all obligations of group under the agreement. Guarantor hereby agrees that its obligations hereunder shall be unconditional, irrespective of the validity or enforceability of the agreement, the absence of any action to enforce the agreement, the waiver of any rights thereunder, or the amendment of the agreement or any other circumstance which might otherwise constitute a legal or equitable discharge or defense of a guarantor. Guarantor hereby waives diligence, a presentment, demand of performance, any right to require a proceeding first against group, protest or notice with respect to the obligations under this agreement and all demands whatsoever. Guarantor agrees that this guarantee will not be discharged except by complete performance of the obligations contained in this guarantee.

This guarantee shall not be affected by, and shall remain in full force and effect notwithstanding, any bankruptcy, insolvency, liquidation, or reorganization of group or Guarantor.

2. *Representations and Warranties. Guarantor hereby represents, warrants and agrees as follows: (a) Guarantor has all requisite legal power to enter into this guarantee; (b) Guarantor has all requisite legal power to carry out and perform its obligations under the terms of this guarantee; and (c) this guarantee constitutes the legally valid and binding obligation of Guarantor, enforceable in accordance with its terms.*

3. *Governing Law. This guarantee shall be deemed to be a contract made under the laws of the state of Florida and shall for all purposes be governed by and construed in accordance with the laws of such state.*

IN WITNESS WHEREOF, Guarantor has executed this guarantee as of the date first above written. (Signatures and Date follow).

Would the payor be likely to change any of the foregoing language? Not hardly!

My suggestion is to have this plan ready before entering negotiations with any payor so that the time frame of the negotiation can be moved along in due course without delay. This is part of your organization development work. Do not be caught without having thought it through and establishing a viable plan.

12 CHAPTER

Delegated Utilization and Claims Management for the MSO

In this chapter is a sample of a requirement often seen in managed-care capitated contracts with IPAs and PHOs. Normally, these functions are assumed at the MSO level. I have included a sample exhibit to a network provider contract for you to examine closely so that you can project costs included to be able to service the contract. In the circles that I travel, these two delegated tasks together with enrollment features are worth about 14% to 18% of premium. Typically, the payors reserve upwards of 15% to 20% of premium for these overhead expenses and margins.

Naturally, a fledgling MSO with immature software and systems engineering of a sophisticated Information Systems nature, would not be able to undertake a task this grand without some expertise help that might cost more than the job would pay.

CLAIMS PAYMENT RESPONSIBILITIES (delegated claims payment)

Group shall administer claims for covered services rendered by represented providers in accordance with this exhibit and the terms of the agreement.

1. Group shall administer all claims for covered services in accordance with payor's claim administration standards and any other standards set forth in applicable law, including but not limited to, ERISA. Group agrees to reimburse represented providers for covered services within thirty (30) days of receipt of a properly completed bill for covered services. Payor may withhold all or a portion of group's capitation payment if group repeatedly fails to reimburse represented providers on a timely basis.

2. With reasonable notice, group agrees to allow payor representatives to conduct on-site reviews of group's claims administration facilities. Such reviews shall be for the sole purpose of evaluating group's performance of its claims administration responsibilities under this agreement, including, but nor limited to, ascertaining the quality and timeliness of group's claims processing. Group agrees to correct any deficiencies detected during such reviews within sixty (60) days of payor's submission of a written report detailing such deficiencies.

3. Group shall be responsible for the production of all applicable tax reporting documents (for example, 1099s) for represented providers. Such documents shall be produced in a format and within the time frames set forth in applicable state and federal laws and/or regulations.

4. Group shall ensure that represented providers submit claims for covered services rendered to participants in other programs for which payor has retained claims payment responsibility directly to payor in accordance with the applicable program attachment and program requirements.

5. Group shall produce explanations of benefits for both represented providers and participants. Such explanations of benefits shall be in a format and contain data elements acceptable to payor.

6. Group shall develop and deliver training programs for represented providers which outline group's billing and

reimbursement processes. Group shall make best efforts to ensure that represented providers avoid submitting claims to payor for those covered services rendered to participants for whom group has been delegated claims payment responsibility.

7. Group or its represented providers shall provide payor with encounter data on a weekly basis showing all services provided to each participant for whom group receives capitation payments. Such encounter data shall be submitted in accordance with applicable HMO program requirements and in a format acceptable to payor. Payor may elect to withhold payment of group's compensation if group fails to submit encounter data in accordance with this agreement.

UTILIZATION MANAGEMENT (delegation of utilization management)

1. Group will establish a utilization management program acceptable to payor and in accordance with NCQA standards. Group's utilization management program shall seek to assure that healthcare services provided to participants are medically necessary and will include, but not be limited to the following: management of referrals between the primary care physician and specialist, prior management of inpatient services, discharge planning, major condition case management, and utilization information management.

2. Group shall prepare such periodic reports or other data as requested by payor relating to its utilization management program in a format acceptable to payor.

3. Group shall not materially modify its utilization management program without payor's prior approval.

4. Group agrees to include payor's medical director or medical director designee on group committees which are responsible for the review and continued development of group's utilization management program and other related programs.

5. Payor shall have the right to audit group's utilization management activities upon reasonable prior notice.

Group shall cooperate with any such audits.

6. If payor determines that group cannot meet its utilization management obligations set forth herein, payor may elect to assume responsibility for such activities. If payor elects to assume responsibility for such activities, the parties agree to renegotiate the rams set forth in this agreement to the extent necessary, and group shall cooperate and provide to payor any information necessary to perform such activities.

7. All referrals shall be to represented providers, except where an emergency requires otherwise or in other cases where group's medical director specifically authorizes the referral. Except in an emergency, group shall require all represented providers to obtain authorization from group prior to hospital admission of any participant or outpatient surgical procedures.

8. Group or its represented providers shall provide payor with referral data on a daily or weekly basis showing all services authorized for each participant. Such referral data shall be submitted in accordance with applicable HMO program requirements and in a format acceptable to payor may elect to withhold payment of group's compensation if group fails to submit referral data in accordance with this agreement.

I have found that the most leveraged groups are the proactive networks are well-prepared with reinsurance and errors and omissions coverage who can agree to these terms and conditions. The main reason is that the network retains the data ownership and commensurate power to make good decisions for the group.

13
CHAPTER

Considerations for Reinsurance Purchasing

In a healthcare environment that changes daily, healthcare providers are increasingly exposed to the financial risks associated with providing medical care. As you are probably aware, many medical providers have reimbursement contracts with Managed Care Organizations (MCOs) based upon capitation. Capitated contracts provide for a fixed fee paid by an MCO to a participating healthcare provider. This fixed payment is intended to cover all the expenses associated with the medical needs of the provider's patient population, and remains fixed without regard to the actual cost of medical services required by a patient.

So what does this all mean to healthcare providers? If total patient costs fall below the capitation amount, the provider keeps any excess. But if costs exceed the capitation payments, the provider must absorb the additional costs. Capitation can work well for healthcare providers in providing routine medical care. However, when patients experience medical catastrophes, the capitated provider is exposed to a financial catastrophe. Consider the following:

A teenager was admitted to a hospital after being involved in a car accident, and lapsed into a coma that lasted for an extended period. During this period, the patient required extensive medical care and was kept alive on life-support systems. The patients family was insured through an MCO, which had a capitation arrangement with an Independent Practice Association (IPA) and a Provider Hospital Organization (PHO).

With this arrangement, the payment for the hospital services required by the teen was limited to the fixed monthly capitation payment received by the IPA/PHO. And, because of this, the IPA/PHO had to bear significant excess expenses not paid by the MCO. The resulting out-of-pocket cost to the IPA/PHO was close to $1 million, potentially having a serious impact on the overall financial health of the IPA/PHO.

Covering the Remainder

A majority of healthcare costs stems from a small number of catastrophic cases such as the previous example. In a capitated environment, these cases critically threaten a provider financially. While some MCOs may offer provider excess coverage, providers should consider whether it is wise to seek a financial safety net from the same organization that is the source of the actual financial risk. (I have found very often that indeed they do charge a "convenience" surcharge, although not listed as such, it is reflected in the price quoted.) Obtaining provider excess insurance from a single insurer, distinct from the MCO, separates the financial risks assumed under a capitation arrangement from the source of the basic medical reimbursement. A single insurer also gives providers the opportunity to obtain superior coverage and reduced administrative burdens, often at lower costs than MCO-sponsored programs.

In order to protect themselves against large potential losses, healthcare providers need comprehensive insurance that is both flexible with and responsive to their unique needs. Many vendors can provide this coverage with provider excess loss insurance policies. Their coverage is customized for healthcare providers and designed to cover the excess costs associated with catastrophic medical events. Often policies provide hospitals, physician groups, and other medical practitioners key features, such as coverage for hospitals and professional charges, flexible coinsurance provisions and deductibles, extended reporting periods, as well as additional features that can be tailored to each provider's needs. Most healthcare providers cannot afford to be without coverage, although many in this day and age try to "run bare." It astounds me to think how many capitated providers are seeing 30% of actual billed charges (or less!) when capitated reports are prepared, yet they have not taken the time to investigate the possibility of reinsuring the risks they have assumed.

Catastrophic financial losses for healthcare providers under capitation arrangements can exceed $1,000,000 per patient in any given year. Provider excess loss insurance reimburses providers for catastrophic medical expenses which are not anticipated by the level of capitation payment paid by an MCO. Many policies includes the following key features:

Term of Coverage   Many policies are issued for a twelve-month term and does not need to coincide with the term of the provider service agreement with the MCOs. If your contract is longer, you may want to purchase a longer term policy. However, in my experience, it may pay to have the flexibility of an annually renewed/renegotiated policy that provides the opportunity to buy less coverage and pay less as you become more familiar with capitated management techniques. Most offer monthly premium rates that are guaranteed for the policy period, and can be tailored for coverage to meet the medical risk incurred by the provider under terms of its provider service agreements.

Experience Rating   Newer organizations with little experience in capitated risk management as a group may be rated due to their lack of experience with capitated risk management. Although their underwriting process considers the factors developed through a pricing model, they can also consider prior claims experience in establishing premium rates. Sometimes, underwriters offer an option to structure the policy so that favorable loss experience during the policy term can be shared with the insured upon renewal.

Covered Person   The typical reinsurance policy can cover commercial, Medicare, and Medicaid patients in one contract. However, premiums, deductibles, and coinsurance provisions can vary based on the unique exposures providers face in the demographics of their patient population.

Eligible Expense   Reimbursable expenses reflect services and supplies provided by the insured to patients under the terms of the insured's provider service agreements with MCOs. Coverage for both hospital and professional services is available. Reimbursements can be based on reasonable and customary charges, per diems, or the common reimbursement schedules such as McGraw-Hill, RBRVS, etc. The insurance will not reimburse amounts greater than the insured has actually paid. An actuary can often assist you in the development of internal fee schedule development for an IPA or PHO so that the MSO can manage the capitation and the risk based upon the monthly funding it receives from the health plan, rather than the full premium dollar.

Annual Deductibles   Deductibles are generally per member, per policy year and can be tailored to meet each provider's different needs and ability to assume risk. Deductibles for hospital services can be as low as $25,000 and deductibles for professional charges can start as low as $7500. While standard policies do not provide for a carry forward, some offer a 31-day carry forward provision for hospital coverage.

Coinsurance   Often the policies offer flexible provisions to meet each provider's needs, willingness, and ability to assume financial risk.

Annual Maximum   The typical reinsurance policy defines maximum reimbursement for each individual based on annual limits. Hospital coverage limits are typically $1,000,000 per member, per year, and annual coverage limits for professional services can be up to $250,000.

Benefit Accumulation and Reporting Period   Expenses for eligible claims must be incurred within the 12-month policy term.

Payment and reporting of eligible expenses by the insured can occur from three to six months after the expiration of the policy.

Technical Expertise It is best to seek out a reinsurance broker or underwriter who is skilled in capitated risk analysis. Seek out underwriters who can look beyond stereotypes of distressed industry classes or geographic and economic trends to fully evaluate the individual risk. Look for those who offer customized policies and individually tailored policy endorsements to meet the unique coverage requirements of each healthcare provider.

Stable Capacity The financial strength and stability of a reinsurance company is recognized by the ratings agencies, earning an "A (excellent)" rating from A.M. Best Company, Inc. and a claims-paying ability rating of "A+" from Standard & Poor's.

What to Consider When Buying Capitated Stop Loss/Reinsurance From a Private Insurer

A very helpful article was published in a newsbrief from Healthcare Financial Management Association's Southern California Chapter, written by William D. Dyer, President, Healthcare Plus Insurance Services, Inc., who is a former underwriter and current broker and reinsurance specialist in capitated stop loss/ reinsurance, and Ira J. Forkish, Contributing Editor and Executive Vice President of Healthcare Plus Insurance Services, Inc., also a broker, and a specialist in capitated stop loss/reinsurance. Mr. Forkish is also a member of Managed Care Committee. The article addressed a checklist of concepts to consider when you are new to the business of capitation and purchasing provider excess loss insurance from brokers and vendors.

The article stated, as I believe that most providers intent is to save money and hopefully, buy better or equivalent coverage. When seeking this type of coverage, they stated that there are several things to consider: primarily cost and coverage.

Cost As you are aware, you have two cost categories: (1) In your facility or contracted provider care and (2) out of facility or non-contracted provider care.

When you have a patient in your facility or under the care of a contracted provider, you have greater control over your costs and you should need a minimal reimbursement from stop loss, such as 50% or 45% of billed charges. However, outside your facility or noncontracted providers, you are subject to the good will of your fellow colleagues. Our usual recommendations to our clients regarding the out of facility care is to request a 70% reimbursement or even a 90% reimbursement of the amount that you actually pay that facility or provider.

Coverage Many people approach the question of what level of coverage to purchase from an intuitive standpoint instead of from an analytical one. From my experience, I have learned that intuition was why you took the risk in the first place, in most cases, why not seek the back-up of good analytical/actuarial science by shopping for the coverage based on facts and scientific method. Realize that you are going to a outside insurer and you can design any level of reimbursement, within reason, and any deductible. A good actuary can assist your organization in ascertaining what your real exposure may be, so that your accounting department can determine the projected cost of doing business is and the broker can then design your coverage to reimburse that cost or slightly below it.

Most providers buy coverage from brokers who specialize in this area. The benefits of a qualified broker are the following: Qualified brokers of reinsurance/stop loss assist you in the evaluation and recommendations for the appropriate way of insuring your risk.

If the broker has a substantial book of business with the various insurance companies that are available, they have more clout than you do in terms of receiving competitive pricing and resolving service issues. A "true broker" has the ability to access many different insurance markets, which increases your odds of receiving the best possible value for your premium dollar.

Selection of a broker may or may not come easily. When capitation is popular in a managed care market, providers and identified groups will often receive many mailers or phone calls from various brokers throughout the country who are touting their ability to help them obtain this type of coverage. Markets new to capitation may not be romanced as often, or at all. The first step, if you are in the latter category, is to check your Yellow Pages under "Medical Reinsurance Underwriters." You will see a few listings. Call your professional organizations, the American Hospital Association, and the Healthcare Financial Management Association at (800) 252-HFMA. They may give you leads to begin your query and selection process. Some of the brokers I am familiar with include (in no particular preferential order) Fortis, Alexander and Alexander, Healthcare Plus Insurance Services, Inc., Executive Risk, and others. I will include a directory of where to go for assistance in the appendices of this book to make life a little easier.

A little secret I would like to share with you is that many providers send out their request for quote to every broker who has ever sent them a piece of mail on the subject. Experiences teaches you that this is not the best way to buy this type of coverage. Many of these brokers work with the same insurance companies which results in multiple submissions of your risk to the same underwriters. The underwriter at the insurance company will see that none of the brokers who are involved have control over the account and thus, are in no position to negotiate. The underwriter will feel that he has a great chance of obtaining your account since there are so many people trying to sell his product for him. Consequently, the underwriter will not give you the best deal. They will quote their full retail rates. I find that it is best to select a couple of the most impressive, customer service oriented brokers and have them choose which insurance companies they plan to submit your risk to. Allow each broker to go to two or three insurers exclusively so the underwriters will not receive multiple submissions. I picked up this tip by experience, but Dyer and Forkish also state it in their article. I liken this to selecting a prom dress. You never want to show up at the prom and have three other ladies wearing the same gown! Make sure they do not overlap in who they submit to, do not be shy about asking, and do not be shy about telling them why! It saves everybody time and aggravation and does not let the system get over on you.

In selecting a broker, find a broker who has several verifiable clients who are currently being serviced by the broker. If they do not have at least ten accounts, then consider them fairly new to medical reinsurance. I find it uncanny that sometimes this "stop loss expert" knows less about the excess loss coverage than the client. Also, be careful about going to your current broker or life insurance agent, as sometimes, through their lack of experience and goal-oriented salesmanship, they may accidentally mis-inform you and could do more harm than good. Select a broker who is more than just a order-taker/salesman. The brokers who are technically oriented often receive more respect from underwriters and in turn often receive the best pricing for their clients. Choose a broker that brings added value. If all the broker does is send your submission to an underwriter and comes back with a quotation which he tries to sell you, they have not earned their commission. You want a broker who is going to work with you to design the coverage to your needs, aggressively negotiate your final pricing, make sure that the insurance company pays your claims in a quick and efficient manner, and deliver service after the sale, through his/her availability to answer questions on an ongoing basis as your questions arise, needs change, or risk exposure increases with added managed-care agreements throughout the year.

Look to do business with a true insurance broker, meaning one who has access to various underwriters in your state area. There are many brokers who only represent one or two insurance companies. When you buy coverage from these types of sales people, you are not making a fully-informed decision about what is available in the marketplace. The best way to identify this type of broker is to ask for a minimum of four quotes, if the broker cannot do this for you, he is not a "true broker." If he/she carries some of the same lines as other brokers, that is when you assign them to a specific underwriter so that you do not have the crossover described above.

Many providers purchase stop loss without understanding what they have bought. Look for your broker to assist and educate you in the mechanics of reinsurance and stop-loss coverages. Any broker who will not take the time to educate his/her client may be oriented towards intentionally taking advantage of the policyholder with unanswered questions and vague policy language.

Be careful when going to insurance societies that are outside the rating system of Standard and Poor's and A.M. Best.

Many veterans can recite a tale of woe as they describe numerous stories of dealing with such entities to purchase coverage from a European insurance society that was nonadmitted and not financially rated by the normal rating authorities. They recite stories of how they have been in dispute with the claims organization that was processing this European insurance society claims. Often they are left without proof of coverage from the company, or they have been left with no verifiable documentation of coverage. They tell of tales that include the mishap of only receiving a one page letter from their broker that listed a reimbursement formula that was unintelligible.

When Buying Coverage From an Insurance Company, What Should You Consider?

When you buy a stop-loss/reinsurance policy from an insurance company, obtain a sample of a contract from the insurer. Your claims will not necessarily be paid in accordance with the quotation that the broker gives you. As in all contracts, respect the Entire Agreement paragraph for what it is. Read the entire policy and understand that any verbal, marketing, or other discussions, negotiations, arrangements, or promises are notwithstanding upon your policy unless they are included in the contract. Memorandums of understanding or written or verbal clarifications are not valid unless they are included in an insurance policy as a declaration, schedule, or other recognized and incorporated document.

Have the specimen contract reviewed by your health law attorney to make sure there are not any glaring problems with it. Look for clauses that require timely filing of claims for reporting limits, some are so tight that they reduce the benefit by as much as 50%, though not highlighted in their proposal.

Another techniques is to give all brokers, insurers, or underwriters the same case scenario and have them explain how their company would handle the situation. I am often surprised at the differences in approach as well as the difference in coverage.

Be sure the insurer is "admitted" by the Department of Insurance. Never buy from a "non-admitted" insurer, it is not worth the risk. Check on complaints and problems and perhaps even request or obtain a copy of their annual statement filed with the department each year.

If a broker tries to sell you a non-admitted insurer, strongly consider working with another broker. In many states, including California, the broker is required to have you sign a disclosure statement when selling a non-admitted insurer. If the broker does not voluntarily disclose this information, get a new broker to avoid an unnecessary risk.

Non-admitted insurance companies are not subject to the financial solvency regulation and enforcement which apply to admitted insurance companies. These insurance companies do not participate in any of the insurance guarantee funds created by admitted insurers in your state. Therefore, these funds will not pay your claims or protect your assets if the non-admitted insurance company becomes insolvent and is unable to make payments as promised.

Dealing with Managing General Underwriters (MGUs) Since provider stop loss is a very specialized area of insurance, entrepreneurial underwriting professionals, or MGUs, convince an insurer to allow them to represent their company. The MGUs perform all the major tasks that the insurance company normally does, meaning that they receive premiums, underwrite the risk, pay the claims, and market the product. Most MGUs are very reputable organizations and are a good source to buy this coverage from, but make sure you check them out thoroughly before you buy them. Things to consider when purchasing from a Managing General Underwriter, Dyer and Forkish recommend the following:

> *First,* determine how long has the MGU been in business. If for only three to five years you may be taking a risk. The risk is the MGU collecting all of your premium on behalf of the insurance company. Premium is not paid to the insurance company until the end of the year. If the MGU were to go bankrupt, commit fraud, or not have the ability to pay your claims, you might find yourself uninsured, or in court trying to get your claims paid.

Second, ask what are the finances of the MGU? Again, think of the concerns indicated above. If it is a privately-owned business controlled only by a few individuals, you are taking a risk.

Third, buy only from in-state MGUs. If you ever have a problem you can go to the State Department of Insurance for help. Also, if you need to take legal action it is less expensive and easier to do this against a business in your own state versus out of state.

Fourth, if you get a quotation from a MGU that is dramatically below the other insurers that you received quotes from, you should definitely question the viability of that coverage.

Fifth, ask the MGU to give you a list of insurers they work with and how long they have had that relationship. Be aware of MGU's who change insurance companies every year or two. This could indicate that they are losing money for their insurers and that you are putting yourself at risk to buy from them.

Lastly, just because an insurance company has been convinced by a MGU to allow them to do business on their behalf does not mean that the MGU is a viable organization. Insurance companies are not known to be perfect in their due diligence when it comes to who they do business with. Wise advice indeed!

Proper reinsurance coverage can translate into a six or seven figure reimbursement to your facility, so choose wisely. The good news is that if you are a typical provider with good claims experience you should save anywhere from 30% to 70% over what you have been paying to the HMO. Thus, you will increase your bottomline profits and allow your negotiations with the HMO to be focused solely on your capitation rates and not on stop loss. Without the knowledge of what your reinsurance terms and your actuarial projections are, never negotiate full-risk, capitated agreement dollars. You set yourself up for a loss.

APPENDIX A

MSO Proforma
Budget Worksheet

The following model document is an MSO Budget using hypo-
thetical figures and is strictly illustrative of format and budget
line items to be considered initially. Though not exhaustive and
complete, it should provide the reader with an idea and direction
of how to proceed in the development of their own document.
For the purposes of this presentation, the MSO is to assume that
all the physicians will use the billing and transcription services.
This in turn will mean eliminating other outsourced billing and
transcription. This will also possibly eliminate or leave vacant,
one or more positions within each office. Revenue is assumed
as physican contributions and initial set-up costs and operative
expenses will be offset by these contributions. Revenue in the en-
suing years will be dependent upon the type of products developed by the organization and the reimbursement options selected
by the members. It is reasonable to assume that the operation can
function at break even or better in subsequent years.

   Here are three methods of providing structure for the
Physician contributions.

REVENUE

A. Flat Fee Membership (Low-Risk/Most Conservative)

For the purposes of this revenue variation, it is proposed that all
physicians pay a flat rate of $750 per month per physician, re-
gardless of the amount of billing and transcription services used.

Members	Cost per Member	Total Monthly Revenue	Total Yearly Revenue
$250	$750	$187,500	$2,250,000

B. Flat Fee with Service Utilization Cap (Moderate-Risk Plan)

For the purposes of this revenue variation, it is proposed that all physicians pay a flat fee of $500 per month per physician with a limit to 700 claims per month and 5000 lines transcription per month. If a physician uses more services, the physician will pay a 4% per claim fee-for-service for billing and $0.15 per line fee for service for transcription. 700 claims is based on what most physician sees, on average 35 patients per day and each patient will have a claim whether private pay or insurance and per each patient, approximately 7.14 lines of transcription is dictated per patient encounter. If only 75 physicians did 900 claims a month, averaging $75 per claim, then an extra 1428 lines per month would then be generated. With this assumption then the following would occur:

Members	Cost per Member	Total Monthly Revenue	Total Yearly Revenue
$250	$500	$125,000	$1,500,000
$ 75	$592	$ 44,400	$ 532,800
$ 75	$142	$ 10,710	$ 128,520
Total		$180,110	$2,161,320

C. Pay Per Service (High Risk/Most Liberal)

For the purposes of this revenue variation, it is proposed that all physicians contract the various services at a fee-for-service arrangement, regardless of use, amount generated, or what economic harm to the physician. This also assumes all physicians participate. Billing rates are proposed at a fair market value of 4% per net claim and that the least billed will be $2 per claim and the most to be charged will be $500 per claim. Using statistical averages the following may occur:

Members	4%, Low	Dollar Range, High	Average Dollars	Monthly Revenue	Yearly Revenue
62.5	2.00	$ 25.00	$ 13.50	$ 843.75	$ 10,125.00
62.5	25.01	$150.00	$ 87.50	$ 5468.75	$ 65,625.00
62.5	150.01	$325.00	$237.51	$14,844.38	$178,132.50
62.5	325.01	$500.00	$412.51	$25,781.88	$309,382.50
Total				$46,938.76	$563,265.00

Transcription Rates are proposed at fair market value of $0.12 cents a line. This is also broken down to statistical averages based upon a maximum of 7000 lines. This still uses the same averages as Section B proposes for average transcription lines per claim, etc. Therefore, the possible breakdown may occur:

Members	Transcription, Low	Line Range, High	Average Lines	Monthly Revenue	Yearly Revenue
62.5	1.00	2000	1001	$ 7507.50	$ 90,090.00
62.5	2001.00	4500	3251	$ 24,382.50	$ 292,590.00
62.5	4501.00	6500	5501	$ 41,257.50	$ 495,090.00
62.5	6501.00	7000	6751	$ 50,632.50	$ 607,590.00
				$123,780.00	$1,485,360.00

Total Monthly Proposed Revenue	Total Yearly Proposed Revenue
$170,718.75	$2,048,625.00

Proposed Fixed Costs

Item	Cost	(These figures are based on a non-financed cost)
Legal fees	$28,000.00	This includes $20,000 fee for "non-qualified" SEC filing
Computer hardware	$64,383.13	This is based on Addendum A computer hardware system
Trans./sect. software	$70,850.00	This is based on Addendum E computer software system
E-Z cap billing software	$45,575.00	This is based on Addendum G computer software system
Office equipment	$148,885.00	This is based on Addendum I office equipment list

Costs	Monthly	Yearly	
Salaries	26,425.00	317,100.00	
Business	20,000.00	240,000.00	
Development office	0.00	0.00	Local market conditions
Occupancy supplies	5000.00	60,000.00	
Professional fees	5572.00	66,864.00	
Carrier/postage	4000.00	48,000.00	
Property insurance	0.00	0.00	Local market conditions
General liability insurance	0.00	0.00	Local market conditions
Workmen's comp.	0.00	0.00	Local market conditions
Errors and omission insurance	0.00	0.00	Local market conditions
Professional liability insurance	0.00	0.00	Local market conditions
Dues and subscriptions	1000.00	12,000.00	
Computer hardware service	2100.00	25,200.00	
Computer software service	1200.00	14,400.00	
Personal property taxes	62.50	750.00	
Corporate taxes	200.00	2400.00	
State, local, other taxes	200.00	2400.00	
Phone costs	500.00	6000.00	
Est. mortgage (avg. of all payments)	14,885.51	178,626.12	
Professional assistance	3000.00	36,000.00	
Total	84,145.01	1,009,740.12	

Possible Financial Outcome	Monthly	Yearly
Revenue	187,500.00	2,250,000.00
Cost	151,774,52	1,821,294.24
Gross profit	35,725.48	428,705.76
Legal fund (10%)	3,572.55	42,870.58
Overcost fund (10%)	3,572.55	42,870.58
Net profit	28,580.38	342,964.60

A P P E N D I X B

Volunteer Committee Survey Form

GETTING EVERYBODY TO PITCH IN

In the early days of network development, very few organizations have the money to hire a team of consultants to develop the network hands-on. Most organizations opt for a consultant to lead the committees directors towards a viable end, allowing for the networks' members to pitch in with sweat equity. In order to get everyone to pitch in and create a master logistics list, a form like this one, handed out at the first meeting, may prove as helpful for you as it did for me.

C O M M I T T E E I N T E R E S T S U R V E Y

Physician's Name: _____

Telephone: Office: _____ Home: _____

Specialty: _____

I Have An Interest In Serving On The Following Committees:

_____ Bylaws

_____ Membership   _____ Credentialing

_____ Quality Assurance/Quality Improvement

_____ Utilization Management/Utilization Review

_____ Healthcare Standards/Medical Appropriateness
            Guidelines

_____ Medical Director's Position

_____ Risk Management   _____ Public Relations

_____ Patient Relations   _____ Hospital Relations

_____ Provider Relations   _____ Finance

_____ Budget Committee   _____ Contracting Committee

_____ Business Development   _____ Info Systems/Computer

_____ *I Have No Interest In Serving On Any Committee*

A P P E N D I X   C

LLC Documentation Set

The following document is intended to apprise the person considering an investment in a new entity such as an IPA, PHO, or MSO, etc. of the material risks of the business enterprise as a limited liability corporation.

DOCUMENT PREPARATION CHECKLIST

Before an organization can prepare this document certain types of information must be prepared for the attorney. Give a brief description of the organization, including the following information:

- Type of organization;
- Services to be provided by the IDS;
- Types of persons/entities to which membership is being offered;
- Legal capacity description of a member;
- Knowledge and experience in financial business matters enabling the member to evaluate the merits and the risk of the investment;
- Members ability to bear economic risk of the investment;
- Sample copies of the Articles of Incorporation, Bylaws, Membership Agreements (for example Physician Services Agreement, PHO Participation Agreement, Management Services Agreement, Membership Agreement, etc.);
- Market value and transferability information, as applicable;

- If integration is to be accomplished in stages, describe each stage;
- The benefits of membership in the IDS;
- Obligations of the members; and
- Requirements for membership in the IDS.

MEMBER SUBSCRIPTION AGREEMENT

Note: This is a sample form. Federal and state law will strongly influence what disclosures should be made, and state laws can often vary. Consult experienced health law specialty legal counsel in preparing and subscription agreement to confirm its compliance with all applicable laws.

_____, L.L.C.

[Date]

To: _____, L.L.C.

Ladies and Gentlemen:

This Member Subscription Agreement ("Subscription") sets forth the basic terms under which the undersigned ("Subscriber") will agree to purchase a membership interest ("Membership Interest") in _____, L.L.C. (the "IDS") and participate as a member ("Member") of the IDS.

Below the IDS must customize the document with the following information:

I understand that the IDS is being formed as a [State] limited liability company.

- *Type of IDS (e.g., MSG, PHO, Foundation).*
- *Services to be provided by the IDS.*
- *If integration is to be accomplished in stages, describe each stage.*

- *Benefits of membership in the IDS.*
- *Obligations of members.*
- *Requirements for membership in IDS.*

I hereby acknowledge and confirm that I have been furnished with the following information/document. . . .

> Here again it is necessary to determine (and discuss with competent health law specialty legal counsel) what information the Subscriber needs to enable him/her to make an informed decision with respect to the purchase of a Membership Interest in the IDS. For example:

- *Copies of any agreements Subscriber will be required to sign (e.g., provider services agreement, management services agreement),*
- *Copies of the Articles of Organization and Operating Agreement of the IDS.*
- *Any other pertinent corporate and business information respecting the IDS.*

I further acknowledge and confirm as follows:

> Consider including acknowledgments with respect to any one or more of the following issues, as appropriate for the nature of the IDS:

- *Subscriber has read the documents supplied to him/her by the IDS and has had an opportunity to ask questions of and receive satisfactory answers from the organizers, managers, officers, directors, agents, members and/or other persons associated with the IDS, concerning the terms and conditions of Subscriber's investment.*
- *Subscriber understands that the IDS has no history of operations and earnings and/or that his/her investment in the IDS is speculative and involves a high degree of risk which may result in the loss of the total amount of the investment.*

- *Subscriber acknowledges that no assurances have been made regarding existing or future tax consequences which may affect him/her as a Member of the IDS.*
- *Subscriber has received no representations or warranties from the IDS, the organizers, the managers, any member, director, officer or agent, and, in making this investment decision, he/she is relying solely on the information provided to him/her by the IDS and upon personal investigation.*
- *Subscriber acknowledges that Membership Interests are intended for purchase by persons who have such knowledge and experience in financial and business matters that they are capable of evaluating the merits and risks of the prospective investment. Subscriber (either through personal business and financial experience or through advise of a financial consultant), is capable of evaluating the investment, the IDS, the risks associated with this investment and his/her ability to bear the economic risks of such investment.*
- *Subscriber acknowledgment as to certain securities issues (e.g., neither SEC nor state securities administrator has made fairness determination relating to investment neither SEC nor state securities administrator has or will recommend or endorse any offering of Membership Interests in the IDS, Membership Interests in the IDS are/are not being registered under the Securities Act of 1934, Membership Interests are/are not being registered or otherwise qualified for sale under the "Blue Sky" laws and regulations of [State] or any other state and Membership Interests will/will not be listed on any stock or other securities exchange).*

As discussed in the previous Appendix, discuss with legal counsel whether this membership interest is only being offered to "Accredited Investors" and accordingly whether appropriate representations regarding the subscriber's states as an Accredited Investor should be included.

- *Subscriber understands that the IDS will be a [partnership/corporation] for federal and state income tax purposes.*

> Consult with your tax counsel on whether the limited liability company is being established, for tax purposes, as partnership or as a corporation.

- *Subscriber understands certain other issues relevant or unique to the IDS.*

The foregoing expression of my awareness and understanding relating to the purchase of a Membership Interest in the IDS is true and accurate as of the date of this letter and shall be true and accurate as of the date of issuance of the Membership Interest. If any of the facts stated above shall change in any respect prior to the issuance of the Membership Interest, I will immediately deliver to the Managers a written statement to that effect specifying which information has changed and the reasons therefor.

I hereby covenant and agree as follows:

1. Purchase Price—I hereby agree to Purchase a Membership Interest in the IDS, at a nonrefundable purchase price of ($_____) ("Purchase Price"). In consideration of the purchase and sale of such Membership Interest, I hereby agree to pay to the IDS, upon the IDS's acceptance of this Subscription, the Purchase Price by certified cashier's check made payable to the order of the IDS.
2. [Required Agreements]—I agree to enter into [name] of [agreement(s)] with the IDS.

> Describe the agreements (e.g., management services, provider services) that Subscriber for his/her professional association or partnership) will be required to execute and Subscriber's obligations under the agreements. Consider including the following covenants/agreements:

- *Agreement to pay any fees required under the agreements; and*
- *Consequences of termination or breach of the agreements.*

3. Acceptance of Subscription; Right to Terminate Offer— The [Governing Entity] of the IDS has the right to accept or reject this Subscription and this Subscription shall be deemed to be accepted by the IDS only when it is signed by an authorized representative of the IDS. I agree that Subscriptions need not be accepted in the order they are received, and that if within 30 days after the date of this Subscription ("Offer Period") the IDS has not received at least _____ Subscriptions, then the IDS may terminate this offering and withdraw this offer by written notice to me. Following such termination of this offering, the IDS shall have no further obligations to me. The IDS may, in its sole discretion, extend the Offer Period up to an additional 45 days upon written notice to me. I understand that the IDS will provide written notice to me of its decision to accept or reject my Subscription.

4. Closing—No later than days after I receive notice of the IDS's acceptance of my Subscription, I will execute and deliver to the IDS the following:
   A. [List Required Agreements];
   B. Certified Check or Cashiers Check in the amount of the Purchase Price made payable to the order of the IDS; and
   C. Any other miscellaneous receipts, consents or other documents deemed necessary by the IDS to effect the transactions contemplated in this Subscription.

Upon delivery of executed copies of the above agreements and the Purchase Price to the IDS ("Closing"), the IDS will issue to me a Certificate of Membership Interest. I agree that upon receipt of the Certificate of Membership Interest I will be obligated to and agree to pay . . .

Here it will be necessary to describe any fees in connection with the Required Agreements (e.g. management fee, any fees due in connection with the Physician Service Agreement).

5. Indemnification—I understand that the IDS and the managers/officers/directors will rely upon all representations, warranties and covenants in this letter, and therefore, I hereby agree to indemnify and hold harmless the IDS and each [member, manager, director, officer, employee and/or agent thereof from and against any and all loss, damage or liability due to or arising out of the breach of any such representation, warranty or covenant. All representations, warranties, and covenants contained in this Subscription and the indemnification contained in this paragraph 5, will survive the acceptance of this Subscription and my admission as a Member of the IDS.

6. Confidentiality—I agree to hold in confidence and not disclose to any other parties any information or data concerning the IDS supplied to me, except to my lawyers, accountants, employees and other agents, as necessary to evaluate this investment. I agree that this confidentiality obligation will be binding upon me and will continue after the termination of this Subscription, whether or not all of the matters contemplated in this Subscription are consummated.

7. Structure and Operation—I understand certain aspects of the planned structure and operation of the IDS to be as follows:

> Describe, in reasonable detail, aspects of the IDS structure and operation that might impact Subscriber's Investment decision. For example:

- *Capitalization (e.g., initial capital contribution, mandatory capital contribution, optional capital contribution).*
- *Restrictions on transfer or assignment of Membership interest.*
- *Disqualification of Member.*
- *Withdrawal by Member.*
- *IDS's purchase rights (e.g., price and term of pay-out) upon Member disqualification or withdrawal.*

> • *Circumstances under which Subscriber would forfeit all or a significant portion of his/her Membership Interest.*

8. Articles and Regulations [Operating Agreement]—I understand and agree that, in addition to the provisions of this Subscription, my Membership Interest will be subject to and I agree to be bound by the provisions of the Articles of Organization and [Regulations Operating Agreement]

Check with legal counsel to include a description of the appropriate governing documents under the applicable state's limited liability company act.

Date: _____   SUBSCRIBER:

                                        _____
                                        Signature of Subscriber

                                        _____
                                        Printed Name

                                        _____
                                        Address

                                        _____

ACCEPTED BY:
_____, L.L.C.
By: _____

INDEX

ABOUT THE AUTHOR

Maria K. Todd has worked in the healthcare industry for over 20 years and has provided consulting services to group practice organizations, hospitals, and other healthcare providers in many cities throughout the United States. With her multi-focal background and education as a health administrator, health law paralegal, HMO provider relations coordinator, and surgical assistant, she has expertise in full risk capitation, managed-care contracting, negotiating on behalf of providers, and provides specialized consulting in the development and implementation of IPAs, PHOs, and MSOs nationally.

Ms. Todd is a member of the Healthcare Financial Management Association (HFMA), the IPA Association of America (TIPAAA), the American Association of Physician Hospital Organizations (AAPHO), the Medical Group Management Association (MGMA), and the National Health Lawyers Association (NHLA).

Ms. Todd's previous consulting projects have resulted in more than 50 successful organizations nationally for IPAs, PHOs, and MSOs in the medical/surgical, optometric, home care, mental health, physical medicine, and single medical and surgical specialty areas. Most recently, she and her partner have successfully developed the country's first nationwide Complimentary and Alternative Medicine Provider IPA and MSO. Presently, she is President and CEO of HealthPro Consulting Consortium, Inc., a firm specializing in developmental and advisory consulting services to healthcare organizations, other national consulting firms, health law firms, and private practice providers. She is also a principle in the Healthcare Business Institute, a national leader in healthcare consulting and educational services for healthcare executives and professionals. Formerly a part of the McGraw-Hill Healthcare Education Group's seminar team, Ms. Todd speaks before numerous state, national, and local organizations and is available for in-house training sessions on a variety of topics related to managed healthcare, capitation, provider and network contracting, and integrated delivery system development and management. You may reach her at her office in Denver at (303) 750-3524, or via the internet at mktodd@healthprocons.com.